POLITICS AND ECONOMICS OF THE MIDDLE EAST

OMAN

CONDITIONS, ISSUES AND U.S. RELATIONS

POLITICS AND ECONOMICS OF THE MIDDLE EAST

Additional books in this series can be found on Nova's website under the Series tab.

Additional E-books in this series can be found on Nova's website under the E-book tab.

POLITICS AND ECONOMICS OF THE MIDDLE EAST

OMAN

CONDITIONS, ISSUES AND U.S. RELATIONS

SEBASTIAN HAAS
EDITOR

New York

Copyright © 2013 by Nova Science Publishers, Inc.

All rights reserved. No part of this book may be reproduced, stored in a retrieval system or transmitted in any form or by any means: electronic, electrostatic, magnetic, tape, mechanical photocopying, recording or otherwise without the written permission of the Publisher.

For permission to use material from this book please contact us:
Telephone 631-231-7269; Fax 631-231-8175
Web Site: http://www.novapublishers.com

NOTICE TO THE READER

The Publisher has taken reasonable care in the preparation of this book, but makes no expressed or implied warranty of any kind and assumes no responsibility for any errors or omissions. No liability is assumed for incidental or consequential damages in connection with or arising out of information contained in this book. The Publisher shall not be liable for any special, consequential, or exemplary damages resulting, in whole or in part, from the readers' use of, or reliance upon, this material. Any parts of this book based on government reports are so indicated and copyright is claimed for those parts to the extent applicable to compilations of such works.

Independent verification should be sought for any data, advice or recommendations contained in this book. In addition, no responsibility is assumed by the publisher for any injury and/or damage to persons or property arising from any methods, products, instructions, ideas or otherwise contained in this publication.

This publication is designed to provide accurate and authoritative information with regard to the subject matter covered herein. It is sold with the clear understanding that the Publisher is not engaged in rendering legal or any other professional services. If legal or any other expert assistance is required, the services of a competent person should be sought. FROM A DECLARATION OF PARTICIPANTS JOINTLY ADOPTED BY A COMMITTEE OF THE AMERICAN BAR ASSOCIATION AND A COMMITTEE OF PUBLISHERS.

Additional color graphics may be available in the e-book version of this book.

Library of Congress Cataloging-in-Publication Data

ISBN: 978-1-62948-086-2

Published by Nova Science Publishers, Inc. † New York

CONTENTS

Preface		**vii**
Chapter 1	Oman: Reform, Security, and U.S. Policy *Kenneth Katzman*	**1**
Chapter 2	Oman 2012 Human Rights Report *U.S. Department of State*	**29**
Chapter 3	Oman 2012 International Religious Freedom Report *U.S. Department of State; Bureau of Democracy,* *Human Rights and Labor*	**57**
Chapter 4	2013 Investment Climate Statement: Oman *Bureau of Economic and Business Affairs*	**63**
Chapter 5	Oman Country Profile *U.S. Department of State*	**89**
Index		**103**

PREFACE

This book examines current conditions, issues and U.S. relations with the country of Oman with a focus on human rights; international religious freedom; investment climate; and a country profile.

Chapter 1 – Prior to the wave of Middle East unrest that began in 2011, the United States had consistently praised the Sultan of Oman, Qaboos bin Sa'id Al Said, for gradually opening the political process without evident public pressure to do so. The liberalization has, to date, allowed Omanis a measure of representation but has not significantly limited Qaboos' role as paramount decision-maker. The modest reforms have not satisfied some Omani civil society leaders, youths, and others, and this disappointment produced protests in several Omani cities in 2011. The domestic popularity of Qaboos, some additional economic and political reform measures, and repression of protest actions, caused the unrest to subside in 2012. High turnout in the October 15, 2011, elections for the lower house of Oman's legislative body suggested that unrest—and the accelerated reforms launched in response—were producing a new public sense of activism, although with public recognition that reform will continue to be gradual. The first-ever municipal elections in Oman on December 22, 2012 furthered the sense of political empowerment among the electorate.

Perhaps because Oman is a long-time U.S. ally in the Persian Gulf, the Obama Administration did not alter policy toward Oman even though some of the 2011-2012 protests were suppressed and activists were arrested. Oman was the first Persian Gulf state to formally allow the U.S. military to use its military facilities, despite the sensitivities in Oman about a visible U.S. military presence there. It hosted U.S. forces during every U.S. military operation in and around the Gulf since 1980 and has become a significant buyer of U.S. military equipment, moving away from its prior reliance on

British military advice and equipment. Oman is also a partner in U.S. efforts to counter the movement of terrorists and pirates in the Persian Gulf and Arabian Sea. It has consistently supported U.S. efforts to achieve a Middle East peace by publicly endorsing peace treaties reached and by occasionally meeting with Israeli leaders in or outside Oman. It was partly in appreciation for this alliance that the United States entered into a free trade agreement (FTA) with Oman, which is also intended to help Oman diversify its economy to compensate for its relatively small reserves of crude oil.

The one significant difference between the United States and Oman on regional issues is Iran. Unlike most of the other Persian Gulf monarchies, Oman does not perceive a major potential threat from Iran. Sultan Qaboos has consistently maintained ties to Iran's leaders, despite the widespread international criticism of Iran's nuclear program and foreign policy. However, successive U.S. Administrations have generally refrained from criticizing the Iran-Oman relationship, perhaps in part because Oman has sometimes been useful as an intermediary between the United States and Iran. Oman played the role of broker between Iran and the United States in the September 2011 release of two U.S. hikers from Iran after two years in jail there, and it reportedly is involved in efforts to obtain the release of other U.S. citizens imprisoned in Iran or in territory under Iran's control.

Chapter 2 – The Sultanate of Oman is ruled by a hereditary monarchy. Sultan Qaboos al-Said has ruled since 1970. The sultan has sole authority to enact laws through royal decree, although ministries draft laws and citizens provide input through the bicameral Majlis Oman (Oman Council). The Majlis is composed of the Majlis al- Dawla (State Council), whose 83 members are appointed by the sultan, and the elected, 84-member Majlis al-Shura (Consultative Council). The last elections took place on December 22 when citizens chose among 1,600 candidates to elect 192 citizens to seats in 11 municipal councils. The 29-member Council of Ministers, selected by the sultan, advises him on government decisions. In 2011 a new law granted the Oman Council powers that expanded its policy review function to include approving, rejecting, and amending legislation and convoking ministers of agencies that provide direct citizen services. Security forces report to civilian authorities.

The principal human rights problems were the inability of citizens to change their government, limits on freedom of speech and assembly, and discrimination against women, including political and economic exclusion based on cultural norms. Thirty-two individuals were convicted on charges of libel against the sultan during the year, receiving prison sentences from six to

18 months and fines of 500 to 1,000 Omani rials (approximately $1,300 to $2,600). Another 12 individuals were convicted on charges of illegal assembly (assembly without a permit) while peacefully protesting some of the libel convictions. The protesters each received a prison sentence of one year and a 1,000 rial fine (approximately $2,600).

Other ongoing concerns included lack of independent inspections of prisons and detention centers, restrictions on press freedom, instances of domestic violence, and instances of foreign citizen laborers placed in conditions of forced labor or abuse.

Security personnel and other government officials generally were held accountable for their actions. The Head of Finance of the Royal Oman Police (ROP) was prosecuted, sentenced, and jailed for four-and-a-half years for embezzlement of over 700,000 Omani rials (approximately $1.8 million). In a separate case, after security forces shot and killed a protester in 2011, authorities conducted an investigation but held no one liable.

Chapter 3 – The Basic Law prohibits discrimination based on religion and protects the right to practice religious rites on condition that doing so does not disrupt public order and, in practice, the government generally enforced these protections. The trend in the government's respect for religious freedom did not change significantly during the year. The Basic Law declares that Islam is the state religion and that Sharia (Islamic law) is the basis of legislation, although legislation is largely based on civil code. The government inconsistently enforced existing legal restrictions on the right to collective worship.

There were no reports of societal abuses or discrimination based on religious affiliation, belief, or practice. U.S. embassy officials regularly met with officials at the Ministry of Endowment and Religious Affairs (MERA) to discuss the expansion of worship space for non-Muslim religious communities. The ambassador established relationships with leaders of religious groups in the country and encouraged the interfaith policies of the government. Embassy staff spoke regularly with minority religious groups, and attended government and community interfaith and religious community events.

Chapter 4 – Report of Bureau of Economic and Business Affairs on 2013 Investment Climate Statement: Oman, dated February 2013.

Chapter 5 – Statement of U.S. Department of State on Oman Country Profile, dated January 5, 2012.

In: Oman: Conditions, Issues and U.S. Relations   ISBN: 978-1-62948-086-2
Editor: Sebastian Haas   © 2013 Nova Science Publishers, Inc.

Chapter 1

OMAN: REFORM, SECURITY, AND U.S. POLICY[*]

Kenneth Katzman

SUMMARY

Prior to the wave of Middle East unrest that began in 2011, the United States had consistently praised the Sultan of Oman, Qaboos bin Sa'id Al Said, for gradually opening the political process without evident public pressure to do so. The liberalization has, to date, allowed Omanis a measure of representation but has not significantly limited Qaboos' role as paramount decision-maker. The modest reforms have not satisfied some Omani civil society leaders, youths, and others, and this disappointment produced protests in several Omani cities in 2011. The domestic popularity of Qaboos, some additional economic and political reform measures, and repression of protest actions, caused the unrest to subside in 2012. High turnout in the October 15, 2011, elections for the lower house of Oman's legislative body suggested that unrest—and the accelerated reforms launched in response—were producing a new public sense of activism, although with public recognition that reform will continue to be gradual. The first-ever municipal elections in Oman on December 22, 2012 furthered the sense of political empowerment among the electorate.

---

[*] This is an edited, reformatted and augmented version of Congressional Research Service, Publication No. RS21534, dated July 12, 2013.

Perhaps because Oman is a long-time U.S. ally in the Persian Gulf, the Obama Administration did not alter policy toward Oman even though some of the 2011-2012 protests were suppressed and activists were arrested. Oman was the first Persian Gulf state to formally allow the U.S. military to use its military facilities, despite the sensitivities in Oman about a visible U.S. military presence there. It hosted U.S. forces during every U.S. military operation in and around the Gulf since 1980 and has become a significant buyer of U.S. military equipment, moving away from its prior reliance on British military advice and equipment. Oman is also a partner in U.S. efforts to counter the movement of terrorists and pirates in the Persian Gulf and Arabian Sea. It has consistently supported U.S. efforts to achieve a Middle East peace by publicly endorsing peace treaties reached and by occasionally meeting with Israeli leaders in or outside Oman. It was partly in appreciation for this alliance that the United States entered into a free trade agreement (FTA) with Oman, which is also intended to help Oman diversify its economy to compensate for its relatively small reserves of crude oil.

The one significant difference between the United States and Oman on regional issues is Iran. Unlike most of the other Persian Gulf monarchies, Oman does not perceive a major potential threat from Iran. Sultan Qaboos has consistently maintained ties to Iran's leaders, despite the widespread international criticism of Iran's nuclear program and foreign policy. However, successive U.S. Administrations have generally refrained from criticizing the Iran-Oman relationship, perhaps in part because Oman has sometimes been useful as an intermediary between the United States and Iran. Oman played the role of broker between Iran and the United States in the September 2011 release of two U.S. hikers from Iran after two years in jail there, and it reportedly is involved in efforts to obtain the release of other U.S. citizens imprisoned in Iran or in territory under Iran's control.

INTRODUCTION

Oman is located along the Arabian Sea, on the southern approaches to the Strait of Hormuz, across from Iran. Except for a brief period of Persian rule, Omanis have remained independent since expelling the Portuguese in 1650. The Al Said monarchy began in 1744, extending Omani influence into Zanzibar and other parts of East Africa until 1861. A long-term rebellion led by the imam of Oman, leader of the Ibadhi sect (neither Sunni or Shiite and widely considered "moderate conservative") ended in 1959; Oman's population is 75% Ibadhi. Sultan Qaboos bin Sa'id Al Said, born in November

1940, is the eighth in the line of the monarchy; he became sultan in July 1970 when, with British support, he forced his father to abdicate.

The United States signed a treaty of friendship with Oman in 1833, one of the first of its kind with an Arab state. This treaty was replaced by the Treaty of Amity, Economic Relations, and Consular Rights signed at Salalah on December 20, 1958. Oman sent an official envoy to the United States in 1840. A U.S. consulate was maintained in Muscat during 1880-1915, a U.S. embassy was opened in 1972, and the first resident U.S. Ambassador arrived in July 1974.

Oman opened its embassy in Washington in 1973. Sultan Qaboos was accorded a formal state visit in April 1983 by President Reagan. He had previously had a U.S. state visit in 1974. President Clinton visited briefly in March 2000.

Table 1. Some Key Facts on Oman

Population	3.15 million, which includes 577,000 non-citizens
Religions	Ibadhi Muslim, 75%; other, 25% (Sunni Muslim, Shiite Muslim, Hindu)
GDP (purchasing power parity, PPP)	$90.6 billion (2012)
GDP per capita (PPP)	$28,500 (2012)
GDP Real Growth Rate	5% (2012)
Unemployment Rate	15%
Inflation Rate	3.5% (2012)
Oil Production	863,000 barrels per day
Oil Reserves	5 billion-5.5 billion barrels
Oil Exports	750,000 barrels per day (bpd)
Natural Gas Production	875 billion cubic feet/yr
Natural Gas Reserves	30 trillion cubic feet
Natural Gas Exports	407 billion cubic feet/yr
Foreign Exchange and Gold Reserves	$15.9 billion (end of 2012)
Energy Structure	Petroleum Development Oman (PDO) controls most oil and natural gas resources. PDO is a partnership between the Omani government (60%), Royal Dutch Shell (34%), Total (4%), and Partx (2%). Oman Oil Company is the investment arm of the Ministry of Petroleum.

Sources: CIA, *The World Factbook*; Energy Information Administration Country Analysis Brief. 2013.

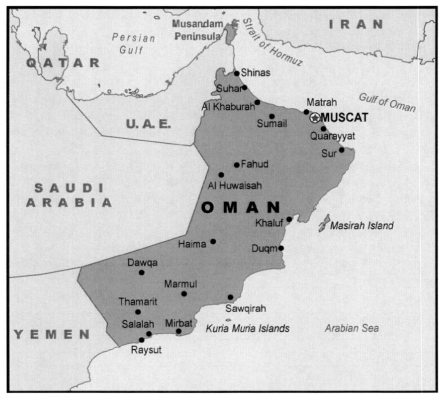

Source: CRS.

Figure 1. Map of Oman.

DEMOCRATIZATION, HUMAN RIGHTS, AND UNREST[1]

Oman remains a monarchy in which decision-making still is largely concentrated with Sultan Qaboos, even though he has a reputation for benevolence and has been considered highly popular. Along with political reform issues, the question of succession had long been central to observers of Oman. Qaboos' brief marriage in the 1970s produced no children, and the Sultan, who was born in November 1940, has no heir apparent. According to Omani officials, succession would be decided by a "Ruling Family Council" of his relatively small Al Said family (about 50 male members). According to these officials, the family might base its succession decision on a sealed

Qaboos letter recommending a successor to be opened upon his death; there are no confirmed accounts of whom Qaboos has recommended. Reported front-runners as successor are Minister of Heritage and Culture Sayyid Haythim bin Tariq Al Said, although some assess him as indecisive, or his older brother, Asad bin Tariq Al Said, a businessman who holds the title of "Representative of the Sultan." Still others say that logical choices include Thuwayni bin Shihab Al Said, the "Special Representative" of the Sultan, or deputy Prime Minister for Cabinet Affairs Fahd bin Mahmud Al Said. The latter is referred to by many Omanis as Prime Minister,[2] although Qaboos himself holds this position, as well as the positions of Foreign Minister and Defense Minister. Some are reportedly pressing Qaboos to name a Prime Minister, and some suggest the secretary general of the Foreign Ministry, Sayyid Badr bin Hamad Albusaidi, as a possibility for such a post; he is said to be efficient and effective.[3]

Despite the three-decade-long opening of the political process discussed below, in recent years some Omanis, particularly younger, well-educated professionals, have come to consider the pace of liberalization too slow. Many older Omanis, on the other hand, tend to compare the current degree of "political space" favorably with that during the reign of the Sultan's father— an era in which Omanis needed the Sultan's approval even to wear spectacles, for example. Among those who have been critical of the pace of political liberalization, some Omanis, including some within the government, note that many top positions have been filled in recent years by former security officials, replacing academics or other professionals. However, evidence that the pace of change has been perceived as slow was demonstrated in 2011-12 in the form of protest in several cities, following unrest sweeping other parts of the region.

Representative Institutions and Election History

Prior to the 2011 unrest, many Omanis and international observers had praised Sultan Qaboos for creating legislative institutions and an election process long before there was any evident public pressure to do so, even though the process advanced incrementally. Under a 1996 "Basic Law," Qaboos created a bicameral "legislative" body called the Oman Council— consisting of an elected Consultative Council (*Majlis As Shura*), and an appointed State Council (*Majlis Ad Dawla*). The Consultative Council was first established in November 1991, replacing a 10-year-old advisory council, and had an initial size of 59 seats. It has been gradually expanded and now has 84 elected members. The Sultan appoints the Consultative Council president from among the membership, and the Consultative Council chooses two vice presidents. The State Council, which had 53 members at inception, has been expanded to 83 appointed members, as of 2013. By law, the appointed State Council cannot have a membership that exceeds the number of elected members of the Consultative Council. The State Council appointees are former high-ranking government officials (such as ambassadors), military officials, tribal leaders, and other notables.

The Oman Council's scope of authority has long been constrained. When it was created, it was not given power to draft legislation, lacked binding power to overturn the sultan's decrees or government regulations, and was generally confined to economic and social issues. Within the Oman Council, the State Council serves as a further check and balance on actions by the Consultative Council, although some believe it acted to limit impulsive excess of the elected body. Prior to the outbreak of unrest in Oman in 2011, some Omanis were saying in interviews that the Oman Council's influence over policy had not increased over time—and many experts assessed that Oman had begun to substantially lag several other Gulf states on political liberalization. As in the other Gulf states, formal political parties are not allowed. Unlike Bahrain or Kuwait, there are not well-defined "political societies" (de-facto parties) in Oman that compete within or outside the electoral process.

Early Electoral History: 1994-2007

Beyond expanding the size of the two chambers, Qaboos has gradually enfranchised Omanis to select the membership of the elected Consultative Council. In the 1994 and 1997 selection cycles for the council, "notables" in each of Oman's districts chose up to three nominees, with Qaboos making a final selection for the council. The first direct elections to it were held in September 2000 (then a three-year term), but the electorate was limited (25% of all citizens over 21 years old). In November 2002, Qaboos extended voting rights to all citizens, male and female, over 21 years of age, and the October 4, 2003, Consultative Council elections—in which 195,000 Omanis voted (74% turnout)—resulted in a council similar to that elected in 2000, including the election of the same two women as in the previous election (out of 15 women candidates).

In the October 27, 2007, election (after changing to a four-year term), Qaboos allowed public campaigning. Turnout among 388,000 registered voters was 63%, including enthusiastic participation by women, but none of the 21 female candidates (out of 631 candidates) won.

2011 Unrest: Dissatisfaction but Not Hunger for a New Regime

Despite the gradual expansion of the electoral process, evidence appeared in 2011 that many Omanis are dissatisfied with the pace of political change and the government's economic performance. About two weeks after Egyptian protests toppled President Hosni Mubarak in February 2011, protests broke out in the northern industrial town of Sohar, Oman. On February 27, 2011, several hundred demonstrators gathered there demanding better pay and more job opportunities; one was killed when security forces fired rubber bullets. Protests expanded in Sohar over the next few days, and spread to the capital, Muscat. Although most protesters said their demonstrations were motivated by a lack of available good jobs, some said they wanted the powers of the Majles expanded to approximate those of a Western legislature. Few, if any, called for Qaboos to step down, even after the deaths of some protesters. Some protesters displayed posters with his picture. Protests continued in Sohar and in Muscat throughout March 2011, including establishment of an encampment in Sohar's main square.

Reforms Intended to Address Dissent

The government calmed some of the unrest through a series of measures, including clearing protesters from Sohar. Not relying solely on repressive measures, the government enacted some reforms: on March 7, 2011, Qaboos shuffled the cabinet by appointing several members of the elected Consultative Council as ministers. An additional woman (Madiha bint Ahmad bin Nasser) was named to the cabinet (education minister). On March 13, 2011, Qaboos issued a decree stating intent to grant the Oman Council legislative and regulatory powers, with exact powers to be determined by a government-appointed committee. Qaboos also sent representatives to meet with protesters, ordered that 50,000 new public sector jobs be created immediately, raised the minimum wage by about one-third (to about $520 per month), and ordered that about $400 be given to unemployed job seekers. He also decreed that the office of public prosecutor will have independence from government control, that there will be new consumer protections, and, as noted below, expanded the powers of the Oman Council. These moves followed an earlier mandated increase in private sector minimum wages of 43% at the beginning of February.

Despite the modest reforms and the security measures, tensions remained high. One demonstrator was killed in a demonstration in Sohar on April 1, 2011. On April 7, 2011, a small group of protesters outside the Oman Council headquarters in Muscat called for an investigation of the security forces for that death and two previous protester deaths. Activists using social media called for protests in Sohar on April 8, 2011, but a heavy security presence prevented fresh protests. During April and May 2011, protests, some large, were held after each Friday's prayers in the city of Salalah. Salalah is the capital of the Dhofar region, which was in rebellion against the Omani central government until the mid-1970s. Protests have been relatively few, but not absent, since. Taking additional steps to address economic concerns, in August 2011, the government increased spending by 9% in 2012 to finance construction projects and more jobs for nationals. A freeze on prices of certain goods, imposed August 18, 2011, could also have been intended to dampen further unrest.

October 2011: Election As the Unrest Abates

The unrest affected the October 2011 Consultative Council elections. The enhancement of the Oman Council's powers, discussed above, raised the stakes for candidates and voters in the Consultative Council elections and State Council appointments, because the next Oman Council would presumably have increased influence on policy. The election date was set as October 15, 2011. Attracted by the enhanced powers of the Oman Council, a total of 1,330 candidates announced their candidacies—a 70% increase from the number of candidates in the 2007 vote. A record 77 women filed candidacies, compared to the 21 that filed in the 2007 vote. The government did not permit outside election monitoring.

Of the 520,000 Omanis who registered to vote, about 300,000 voted—the turnout of about 60% (about the same as in the 2007 election) appeared to refute those who felt that the citizenry would shun the political process following the months of unrest. Hopes among many Omanis that at least several women would win were dashed—only one was elected, a candidate from Seeb (suburb of the capital, Muscat). Some reformists were heartened by the election victory of two political activists—Salim bin Abdullah Al Oufi, and Talib Al Maamari, an academic. The government hailed the turnout as evidence of its popularity and an endorsement of its handling of the 2011 protest movement. There was a vibrant contest for the speakership of the Consultative Council, and the position was won by Khalid al-Mawali, a relatively young entrepreneur. In the State Council appointments that followed the Consultative Council elections, the sultan appointed 15 women, bringing the total female participation in the Oman Council to 16 out of 154 total seats—just over 10%.

On October 19, 2011, in implementation of the March 2011 decree, the Sultan formally granted the Oman Council new powers, including approving, rejecting, and amending legislation, and the ability to question ministers who head agencies that provide direct citizen services. However, the expanded powers appear to fall short of what many observers would consider those of a legislature.

Aftermath of the Unrest

Still, some activism continued, triggering government reaction. In January 2012, the government announced plans to boost its expenditures by about 26% to provide for jobs, social security, and unemployment benefits—an apparent further budgetary effort to head off any resurgence of unrest. However, in July 2012, there was a wave of oil sector strikes and further demonstrations in Sohar by recent graduates protesting a lack of job opportunities. Some protesters expressed anger at what they said was a waste of resources in Sultan Qaboos' sending of 100 horses to the Diamond Jubilee celebration of Britain's Queen Elizabeth.

During 2012, at least 50 activists, including journalists and bloggers, were given prison sentences for "defaming the Sultan," "illegal gathering," or violating the country's cyber laws. Twenty-four of them went on a hunger strike in February 2013 to draw attention to their incarceration and in the hopes of persuading Oman's Supreme Court to hear appeals of their cases. In an effort to achieve reconciliation, on March 21, 2013, the Sultan pardoned 35 of these activists and they were released from prison. International human rights groups praised the pardon, which contrasts sharply with continued arrests and prosecutions of social media activists and others in the other Gulf monarchy states. However, 14 remaining in jail for the Sohar protests went on a hunger strike in March 2013. Also in March 2013, the government announced a limitation on the number of foreign workers and a sharp raise in the minimum wage for Omani workers.

December 2012 Municipal Elections

In its efforts to reduce unrest the government also began a separate electoral process for municipal councils. The councils make recommendations to the government on development projects, but do not make final funding decisions. Previously, only one municipal council was established, for the capital region, and it was all-appointed. On November 15, 2012, the government announced that it would hold the first-ever elections for municipal councils in all 11 provinces—to take place on December 22, 2012. The total number of seats up for election was 192. More than 1,600 candidates registered to run, including 48 women. Four women were elected.

U.S. Responses

The U.S. reaction to the unrest in Oman has been muted, possibly because Oman is a key ally of the United States and perhaps because the unrest appeared minor relative to the rest of the region. No U.S. statements were issued about Oman's responses to the unrest. On June 1, 2011, after the unrest had begun, and after some government force had suppressed protests, then U.S. Ambassador Richard Schmierer told an Omani paper: "...The entire region, including Oman, has witnessed enormous change in an extremely brief period of time. Sultan Qaboos was quick to recognize and respond to the needs of Omanis. The way in which he responded to the concerns of the Omani people is a testament to his wise leadership."[4] At her confirmation hearings on July 18, 2012, after the unrest had mostly ended, Ambassador-Designate to Oman Greta Holz (subsequently confirmed) said "If confirmed, I will encourage Oman, our friend and partner, to continue to respond to the hopes and aspirations of its people."

Broader Human Rights Issues

The government's practices on numerous other issues affect popular sentiment in Oman. The State Department human rights report for 2012 did not repeat the assertions of the reports prior to 2011 that "the government generally respect[s] the human rights of its citizens." The 2012 report repeated the assertions of the 2011 report that the principal human rights problems were the inability of citizens to change their government, limits on freedom of speech and assembly, and discrimination against women, including that based on cultural norms. The 2012 report stated that security personnel and other officials were generally held accountable for their actions. Oman has an appointed National Human Rights Commission which is an "autonomous body" attached to the State Council; it was set up in November 2008.

U.S. funds from the Middle East Partnership Initiative and the Near East Regional Democracy account (both State Department accounts) have been used to fund civil society and political process strengthening, judicial reform, election management, media independence, and women's empowerment. In 2011, Oman established a new scholarship program through which at least 500 Omanis have enrolled in higher education in the United States. Some MEPI funds are also used in conjunction with the U.S. Commerce Department to improve Oman's legislative and regulatory frameworks for business activity.

Freedom of Expression/Media

The State Department 2012 human rights report stated that the law provides for limited freedom of speech and press, but the government generally does not respect these rights in practice. Press criticism of the government is tolerated, but criticism of the Sultan (and by extension, government officials in general) is not. Private ownership of radio and television stations is not prohibited, but there are very few privately owned stations, with the exception of Majan TV, and three radio stations: HiFM, HalaFM, and Wisal. However, availability of satellite dishes has made foreign broadcasts accessible to the public. There are some legal or practical restrictions to Internet usage, and only about 15% of the population has subscriptions to Internet service. Many Internet sites are blocked, primarily for offering sexual content, but many Omanis are able to bypass restrictions by accessing their Internet over smart cell phones. As noted above, some bloggers and other activists who use social media have been prosecuted as part of the government's strategy of reducing public unrest.

Labor Rights

Omani workers have the right to form unions and to strike. However, only one federation of trade unions is allowed, and the calling of a strike requires an absolute majority of workers in an enterprise. The labor laws permit collective bargaining and prohibit employers from firing or penalizing workers for union activity. Labor rights are regulated by the Ministry of Manpower.

Religious Freedom

The 1996 Basic Law affirmed Islam as the state religion, but provides for freedom to practice religious rites as long as doing so does not disrupt public order. The State Department's religious freedom report for 2012 noted no "significant" change of the "trend" in the government's respect for religious freedom and no "reports of societal abuses or discrimination based on religious affiliation, belief, or practice" during 2012. Non-Muslims are free to worship at temples and churches built on land donated by the Sultan, but there are some limitations on non-Muslims' proselytizing and on religious gatherings in other than government-approved houses of worship.

All religious organizations must be registered with the Ministry of Endowments and Religious Affairs (MERA). Among non-Muslim sponsors recognized by MERA are the Protestant Church of Oman; the Catholic Diocese of Oman; the al Amana Center (interdenominational Christian); the Hindu Mahajan Temple; and the Anwar al-Ghubairia Trading Co. Muscat (for the Sikh community). The government agrees in principle to allow Buddhists to hold meetings if they can find a corporate sponsor. Members of all religions and sects are free to maintain links with coreligionists abroad and travel outside Oman for religious purposes. Private media have occasionally published anti-Semitic editorial cartoons.

Advancement of Women

Throughout his tenure, Sultan Qaboos has spoken regularly on the equality of women and their importance in national development, and they now constitute over 30% of the workforce. The first woman of ministerial rank in Oman was appointed in March 2003, and since 2004, there have been several women of that rank. There are two female ministers in the 29-member cabinet (minister of education, and minister of higher education). In April 2004, Qaboos placed five women among the 29 appointees to the public prosecutor's office. Oman's ambassadors to the United States and to the United Nations are women.

There were 14 women in the 2007-2011 State Council, appointed following the 2007 election, up from nine in the 2003-2007 council. Qaboos named 15 women to the State Council that was appointed after the October 2011 Consultative Council election. One woman was elected to Consultative Council in that vote, following a four year period (2007-2011) in which no females served in the elected body. Two women had been chosen in the election cycles prior to 2007.

At the citizen level, allegations of spousal abuse and domestic violence are fairly common, with women finding protection primarily through their families. Omani women also continue to face social discrimination often as a result of the interpretation of Islamic law. On April 9, 2013, one member of the Shura Council tabled a motion to amend the country's laws in order to give nationality to children born to Omani women who are married to a non-national man. Currently, Omani nationality can be passed on only by a male Omani parent.

Trafficking in Persons

In October 2008, President Bush directed (Presidential Determination 2009-5) that Oman be moved from "Tier 3" on trafficking in persons (worst level, assessed in the June 4, 2008, State Department Trafficking in Persons report on that issue), to "Tier 2/Watch List." That determination was made on the basis of Omani pledges to increase efforts to counter trafficking in persons. Oman's rating was raised to Tier 2 in the 2009 Trafficking in Persons remport, and has remain there since, including in the report for 2013 released on June 19, 2013. The Tier 2 ranking is based on an assessment that Oman is making significant efforts to comply with minimum standards for the elimination of trafficking and on its prosecutions for those trafficking in persons. Still, Oman is considered a destination and transit country for men and women primarily from South and East Asia, in conditions indicative of forced labor.

DEFENSE AND SECURITY TIES

Sultan Qaboos, who is Sandhurst-educated and is respected by his fellow Gulf rulers as a defense strategist, has long seen the United States as the key security guarantor of the region. He also has consistently advocated expanded defense cooperation among the Gulf states. Oman was the first Gulf state to formalize defense relations with the United States after the Persian Gulf region was shaken by Iran's 1979 Islamic revolution, which it was at first feared would spread throughout the Middle East and lead to the downfall of monarchy states there. Oman signed an agreement to allow U.S. forces access to Omani military facilities on April 21, 1980. Three days later, the United States used Oman's Masirah Island air base to launch the failed attempt to rescue the U.S. embassy hostages in Iran. During the September 1980–August 1988 Iran-Iraq War, the United States built up naval forces in the Gulf to prevent Iranian attacks on international shipping. Oman played the role of quiet intermediary between the United States and Iran for the return of Iranians captured in clashes with U.S. naval forces in the Gulf during that war.

Under the U.S.-Oman facilities access agreement, which was renewed in 1985, 1990, 2000, and 2010, the United States reportedly can use—with advance notice and for specified purposes— Oman's military airfields in Muscat (the capital), Thumrait, and Masirah Island. Some U.S. Air Force equipment, including lethal munitions, has been stored at these bases.[5] During the renewal negotiations in 2000, the United States acceded to Oman's request

14 Kenneth Katzman

that the United States fund a $120 million upgrade of a fourth air base (Khasab) at Musnanah (50 miles from Muscat).[6]

In conjunction with the 2010 renewal, the U.S. military sought to respond to an Omani request to move some U.S. equipment to expanded facilities at Musnanah, from the international airport at Seeb, to accommodate commercial development at Seeb. Conferees on the DOD authorization act for FY2010 (P.L. 111-84) did not incorporate into that law a DOD request for $116 million to carry out that move, on the grounds that U.S. Central Command had not formulated a master plan—or obtained an Omani contribution—for the needed further construction at Musnanah. One complication could be the fact that, according to observers, about 200 British military personnel were moving to Musnanah from Seeb,[7] and it was unclear whether the facility can accommodate both U.S. and British personnel. However, some of the issues were apparently cleared up because the Defense Authorization Act for FY2011 (P.L. 111-383, signed January 7, 2011) authorized $69 million in military construction funding for the Musnanah facility. Perhaps sensing that the Obama Administration was attempting to accommodate the request, the access agreements were renewed in November 2010.[8]

Oman's facilities contributed to U.S. major combat operations in Afghanistan (Operation Enduring Freedom, OEF) and, to a lesser extent, Iraq (Operation Iraqi Freedom, OIF), even though Omani leaders said that invading Iraq could "incite revenge" against the United States in the Arab world. According to the Defense Department, during OEF there were about 4,300 U.S. personnel in Oman, mostly Air Force, and U.S. B-1 bombers, indicating that the Omani facilities were used extensively for strikes during OEF. The U.S. military presence in Oman fell to 3,750 during OIF because facilities in Gulf states closer to were used more extensively. Since 2004, there have been small numbers of U.S. military personnel in Oman—less than 200, mostly Air Force.[9] Omani facilities reportedly have not been used for air support operations in either Afghanistan or Iraq since 2004. Unlike Bahrain or UAE, Oman has not contributed personnel to training or military missions in Afghanistan.

Even though the U.S. military presence in Oman is relatively small, some Omani officials want to reduce its visibility further. These officials might assess that the U.S. military presence angers Islamist Omanis, Iran, and members of terrorist groups that operate in the Gulf. Some Omani officials reportedly have discussed with their U.S. counterparts the possibility of relocating U.S. personnel to Masirah Island, which is one of the locations covered under the Access Agreement but which is offshore and sparsely

Oman: Reform, Security, and U.S. Policy

inhabited. On the other hand, Masirah's runway is shorter than that of Thumrait, the main location used by the U.S. Air Force, and some U.S. military officials consider Masirah therefore less suitable. To date, there has not been any announced relocation of U.S. personnel to Masirah.

U.S. Arms Sales and other Security Assistance to Oman[10]

Oman's approximately 45,000-person armed force is the third largest of the Gulf Cooperation Council states (GCC, including Saudi Arabia, Kuwait, UAE, Oman, Bahrain, and Qatar) and is widely considered one of the best trained. However, it is not the best equipped. Using U.S. assistance and national funds, Oman is trying to expand and modernize its arsenal primarily with purchases from the United States. Because of his historic ties to the British military, Qaboos early on relied on seconded British officers to command Omani military services. British officers are now mostly advisory. Much of its arsenal still is British-made, although it is increasingly purchasing U.S. and not British systems.

Arms Purchases by Oman

Oman uses Foreign Military Financing (FMF) and national funds to modernize its forces. Some major U.S. sales to Oman have been expected as part of an estimated $20 billion sales package to the Gulf states under the U.S. "Gulf Security Dialogue" intended to contain Iran, although most of the sales notified thus far are to wealthier GCC states such as Saudi Arabia, UAE, and Qatar.

- *F-16s*: In October 2001, Oman purchased (with its own funds) 12 U.S.-made F16 C/D aircraft from new production. Along with associated weapons (Harpoon and AIM missiles), a podded reconnaissance system, and training, the sale was valued at about $825 million; deliveries were completed in 2006. Oman made the purchase in part to keep pace with its Gulf neighbors, including UAE and Bahrain, that had bought F-16s. The Defense Security Cooperation Agency (DSCA) notified Congress on August 4, 2010, of a potential sale to Oman of up to 18 additional F-16s and associated equipment and support. The sale could be worth up to $3.5 billion to the main manufacturer, Lockheed Martin.[11] Oman signed a contract with Lockheed Martin for 12 of the aircraft in December 2011, with a contract for an additional six still possible. The twelve are to be delivered through 2014. On December 11, 2012, DSCA notified a sale of weapons systems for the F-16, including 27 AMRAAMs, 162 GBU laser-guided bombs, and other weaponry and equipment, with a total estimated value of about $117 million.

- In July 2006, according to the Defense Security Cooperation Agency (DSCA), Oman bought the JAVELIN anti-tank system, at a cost of about $48 million.
- In November 2010, DSCA notified Congress of a possible sale of up to $76 million worth of countermeasures equipment and training to protect the C-130J that Oman is buying from Lockheed Martin under a June 2009 commercial contract. The prime manufacturer of the equipment is Northrop Grumman. Another possible sale of countermeasures equipment —in this case for Oman's aircraft that fly Sultan Qaboos—was notified on May 15, 2013.
- On October 19, 2011, DSCA notified Congress of a potential sale to Oman of AVENGER fire units, Stinger missiles, and Advanced Medium Range Air to Air Missiles (AMRAAMs)—all of which are to help Oman develop a layered air defense system. The total value of the potential sale, including associated equipment and training, is about $1.25 billion.
- On June 13, 2012, DSCA notified a sale of various types of AIM "Sidewinder" air-to-air missiles to modernize Oman's F-16 fleet and enhance its interoperability with U.S. forces.
- On May 21, 2013, Secretary of State John Kerry visited Oman reportedly in part to help finalize a sale to Oman of ground-based air defense systems made by Raytheon.[12] The equipment has an estimated value of $2.1 billion. DSCA has not, to date, made a notification to Congress about the potential sale.

Other Uses for Foreign Military Financing (FMF)

FMF has been used to help Oman purchase several other types of equipment that help Oman secure its borders, operate alongside U.S. forces, and combat terrorism. FMF, recent amounts of which are shown in the table below, has helped Oman buy U.S.-made coastal patrol boats ("Mark V") for anti-narcotics, anti-smuggling, and anti-piracy missions, as well as aircraft munitions, night-vision goggles, upgrades to coastal surveillance systems, communications equipment, and de-mining equipment.

Provision of Excess Defense Articles (EDA)

Oman is eligible for grant U.S. excess defense articles (EDA) under Section 516 of the Foreign Assistance Act. It received 30 U.S.-made M-60A3 tanks in September 1996 on a "no rent" lease basis (later receiving title outright). There have been minor EDA grants since 2000, particularly gear to help Oman monitor its borders and waters and to improve inter-operability with U.S. forces. In 2004, it turned down a U.S. offer of EDA U.S.-made M1A1 tanks, but Oman is believed to still need new armor to supplement the 38 British-made Challenger 2 tanks and 80 British-made Piranha armored personnel carriers Oman bought in the mid-1990s.

Regarding purchases from other countries, in the past three years, Oman has continued to buy some British equipment, including Typhoon fighter aircraft and patrol boats. It has also bought some Chinese-made armored personnel carriers and other gear.

IMET Program

The International Military Education and Training program (IMET) program is used to promote U.S. standards of human rights and civilian control of military and security forces, as well as to fund English language instruction, and promote inter-operability with U.S. forces. Nonproliferation, Antiterrorism, Demining, and Related Programs (NADR) funds are used to help Oman develop controls and train and equip personnel to prevent proliferation and combat terrorism. In FY2011, DOD funds ("Section 1206" funds) were used to help Oman's military develop its counterterrorism capability through deployment of biometric data collection devices. A small portion ($48,000) of the FY2012 funds were used to give a human rights seminar to unit commanders and key staff of Oman's military.

Cooperation Against Islamic Militancy

Since September 11, 2001, Oman has cooperated with U.S. legal, intelligence, and financial efforts against terrorism. According to the State Department report on global terrorism for 2012, released May 30, 2013, Oman was actively involved in preventing terrorists from conducting attacks and using the country for safe haven or transport.[13]

Table 2. Recent U.S. Aid to Oman
(In millions of dollars)

	FY2003	FY2004	FY2005	FY2006	FY2007	FY2008	FY2009	FY2010	FY2011	FY2012	FY2013	FY2014
IMET	0.75	0.83	1.14	1.14	1.11	1.43	1.45	1.525	1.622	1.638	2.05	2.0
FMF	80.0	24.85	19.84	13.86	13.49	4.712	7.0	8.85	13.0	8.0	8.0	8.0
NADR		.40	0.554	0.4	1.28	1.593	0.95	1.655	1.5	1.5	1.0	1.0
1206									0.948			

Note: IMET is International Military Education and Training; FMF is Foreign Military Financing; NADR is Nonproliferation, Anti-Terrorism, De-Mining and Related Programs, and includes ATA (Anti-Terrorism Assistance); EXBS (Export Control and Related Border Security); and TIP (Terrorism Interdiction Program). Numbers for FY2011 reflect final allocations by State Dept. FY2013 and FY2014 figures refer to requested funds.

According to the report, the government reported in its press that several supsected terrorist of the Al Qaeda-affiliate Al Qaeda in the Arabian Peninsula (AQAP) had illegally entered Oman from Yemen, where the group is based. The State Department terrorism report for 2009 credited Oman with convicting and sentencing to life in prison an Omani businessman, Ali Abdul Aziz al-Hooti, for helping to plan terrorist attacks in Oman and for helping to fund a Pakistan-based terrorist group, Lashkar-eTayyiba.

The report for 2012 credited Oman, a member of the Middle East and North Africa Financial Action Task Force, with transparency regarding its anti-money laundering and counterterrorist financing enforcement efforts, and with steady improvement in its legal system related to those efforts. The report noted that the government exercises caution and oversight in its commercial banking sector to prevent terrorists from using Oman's financial system. The report adds that Oman does not permit the use of *hawalas*, or traditional money exchanges in the financial services sector and Oman has on some occasions shuttered *hawala* operations entirely.

Other relatively recent steps include Oman's enactment of a January 2007 law establishing a National Committee for Combating Terrorism, a December 2006 agreement with Saudi Arabia to control cross-border transit, and the establishment of a financial intelligence unit of the Directorate of Financial Crimes of the Royal Omani Police. In September 2008, it strengthened its anti-money laundering program by requiring non-banking establishments to verify the identify of their clients and document financial transactions. In December 2004, the government arrested 31 Ibadhi Muslims (Omani citizens) on suspicion of conspiring to establish a religious state, but Sultan Qaboos pardoned them in June 2005.

On November 22, 2005, Oman joined the U.S. "Container Security Initiative," agreeing to prescreening of U.S.-bound cargo from its port of Salalah for illicit trafficking of nuclear and other materials, and for terrorists. U.S. aid to Oman (NADR funds) help Oman establish effective export controls, sustain its counter-terrorism training capabilities, and control movements of illegal immigrants across its borders. In 2011, Oman bought biometrics and other equipment to better secure its borders and coastline, particularly at night. And, it cooperates with State Department programs (Export Control and Related Border Security, EXBS) on developing and implementing comprehensive strategic export controls.

Cooperation on Regional Issues

Sultan Qaboos has sometimes pursued foreign policies outside an Arab or Gulf consensus, although Oman is an integral part of the Gulf Cooperation Council (GCC). Some of Oman's stances, such as its consistent engagement with Iran, have appeared at odds with both GCC and U.S. policy. Other of its positions, such as on the Arab-Israeli dispute, have been highly supportive of U.S. policy, sometimes to the point of alienating other Arab leaders. Oman has generally been a skeptic of some GCC plans for greater economic and political coordination; it balked at a Gulf state plan to form a monetary union and, as discussed below, opposes a Saudi plan for GCC political unity.

Iran

Of the Gulf states, Oman is perceived as politically closest to and the least critical of Iran. Sultan Qaboos has long maintained that Oman's alliance with the United States and its friendship with Iran are not mutually exclusive. Successive Administrations have refrained from criticizing the Omani position, and have used the Oman-Iran relationship to resolve some U.S.-Iran disputes. Oman was an intermediary through which the United States returned Iranian prisoners captured during U.S.-Iran skirmishes in the Persian Gulf in 1987-1988. A U.S. State Department spokesman publicly confirmed that Oman had played a brokering role the September 2010 release from Iran of U.S. hiker Sara Shourd, reportedly including paying her $500,000 bail to Iranian authorities. Oman similarly helped broker the release one year later of her two hiking companions Josh Fattal and Shane Bauer. It was subsequently reported that a State Department official on Iran affairs had coordinated with Oman and with Switzerland (which represents U.S. interests in Iran) to achieve their release.[14] During his May 2013 visit to Oman, Secretary Kerry reportedly discussed with Qaboos possible Omani help in obtaining the release from Iran of ex-Marine Amir Hekmati, a dual citizen jailed in Iran in August 2011, and retired FBI agent Robert Levinson, who went missing in Iran in 2006 and is believed held by groups under the at least partial control of Iran.

Some accounts say that Oman, over the past three years, has drawn closer to Iran than it has previously—even as the United States and its partners have greatly increased sanctions against Iran over its nuclear program. Sultan Qaboos last visited Tehran in August 2009, his first visit there since the 1979 Islamic revolution. He went forward with the visit even though the June 2009 reelection of President Mahmoud Ahmadinejad was widely challenged in Iran as fraudulent by large numbers of demonstrators in Tehran and in other cities.

To this extent, the Qaboos visit was viewed as a sign that Oman was setting aside the issue of Ahmadinejad's reelection. The speaker of Oman's Consultative Council, Khalid al-Mawali, visited Iran on April 13, 2013 to expand cooperation with Iran's *Majles* (elected parliament).

On August 4, 2010, Oman signed a security pact with Iran, which reportedly commits the two to hold joint military exercises.[15] The United States did not criticize Oman's entry into this pact with Iran, possibly believing that the agreement will not result in much significant new cooperation between the two. The 2010 pact follows an earlier pact, signed in August 2009, that focused on cooperating against smuggling across the Gulf of Oman, which separates the two countries. The Oman-Iran pacts were ratified by Iran's *Majles* (parliament) on December 20, 2010. The two countries have held one joint exercise under the pact, according to U.S. Ambassador to Oman Holz. Oman has long publicly opposed any U.S. attack on Iran's nuclear facilities. At the same time, Oman continues to cooperate with U.S. efforts to contain Iran in the Gulf; for example Oman and all the other GCC states participated in 30-nation U.S.-led mine clearing exercises in the Gulf.

Economically, the two conduct formal trade, supplemented by the informal trading relations that have long characterized the Gulf region. Oman's government is said to turn a blind eye to the smuggling of a wide variety of goods to Iran from Oman's Musandam Peninsula territory. The trade is illegal in Iran because the smugglers avoid paying taxes in Iran, but Oman's local government collects taxes on the goods shipped.[16]

Iran and Oman have jointly developed the Hengham oilfield in the Persian Gulf, and the field came on stream officially on July 11, 2013, producing 22,000 barrels of oil per day, a rate expected to rise to 30,000 barrels per day. The investment is estimated at $450 million, although the exact share of the costs between Iran and Oman is not known. The field also produces natural gas, and it is expected to total 80 million cubic feet per day when fully producing. The two countries have also discussed potential investments to develop Iranian offshore natural gas fields that adjoin Oman's West Bukha oil and gas field in the Strait of Hormuz. The Omani field began producing oil and gas in February 2009. Such joint projects appear to constitute a violation of the Iran Sanctions Act (ISA), but the United States has not sanctioned the Hengham or other Iran-Oman energy projects or otherwise accused Oman of any violations or noncooperation with international sanctions against Iran. Ambassador Holz, at her confirmation hearings on July 18, 2012, said that Oman is "compliant and supportive of the international sanctions on Iran."

Experts try to explain why Oman is not as wary of Iran as are the other GCC states. Oman has no sizable Shiite community with which Iran could meddle in Oman, so the fear of Iranian interference is less pronounced. There are also residual positive sentiments pre-dating Iran's Islamic revolution. Oman still appreciates the military help the Shah of Iran provided in helping end a leftist revolt in Oman's Dhofar Province during 1964-1975. Others attribute Oman's position on Iran to its larger concerns that Saudi Arabia has sought to spread its Wahhabi form of Islam into Oman, and Oman sees Iran as a rival to and potential counterweight to Saudi Arabia.

At times, Oman's attempts to steer a middle ground between Iran and the United States have caused problems for Oman. For example, in April 1980, within days of signing the agreement allowing the United States military to use several Omani air bases, the United States used these facilities—reportedly without prior notification to Oman—to launch the abortive mission to rescue the U.S. Embassy hostages seized by Iran in November 1979.[17] Oman complained to the United States about the lack of prior notification of the mission.

Iraq

On Iraq, and generally in line with other GCC states, Omani officials say that the Omani government and population are dismayed at the Shiite Islamist domination of post-Saddam Iraq and its pro-Iranian tilt. Oman opened an embassy in post-Saddam Iraq but then closed it for several years following a shooting outside it in November 2005. The embassy reopened in 2007 but Oman's Ambassador to Iraq is non-resident. The Ambassador, appointed in March 2012, serves concurrently as Oman's Ambassador to Jordan and is resident there. The shooting wounded four, including an embassy employee. Oman provided about $3 million to Iraq's postSaddam reconstruction, a relatively small amount compared to some of the other Gulf states.

Afghanistan

As noted above, Oman has not sent forces or trainers to Afghanistan, although its facilities have been used by U.S. forces to support operations there. Still, Oman has been engaged on the issue— on February 24, 2011, Oman hosted then Chairman of the Joint Chiefs of Staff Admiral Michael Mullen for meetings with Omani senior defense leaders and discussions there on Afghanistan and Pakistan with Mullen's chief Pakistani counterpart, Chief of Army Staff General Ashfaq Kayani.[18]

Arab-Israeli Issues

On the Arab-Israeli dispute, in a stand considered highly supportive of U.S. policy, Oman was the one of the few Arab countries not to break relations with Egypt after the signing of the Egyptian-Israeli peace treaty in 1979. All the GCC states participated in the multilateral peace talks established by the 1991 U.S.-sponsored Madrid peace process, but only Oman, Bahrain, and Qatar hosted working group sessions of the multilaterals. Oman hosted an April 1994 session of the working group on water and, as a result of those talks, a Middle East Desalination Research Center was established in Oman. Participants in the Desalination Center include Israel, the Palestinian Authority, the United States, Japan, Jordan, the Netherlands, South Korea, and Qatar.

In September 1994, Oman and the other GCC states renounced the secondary and tertiary Arab boycott of Israel. In December 1994, it became the first Gulf state to officially host a visit by an Israeli prime minister (Yitzhak Rabin), and it hosted then Prime Minister Shimon Peres in April 1996. In October 1995, Oman exchanged trade offices with Israel, essentially renouncing the primary boycott of Israel. However, there was no move to establish diplomatic relations. The trade offices closed following the September 2000 Palestinian uprising.

Oman has expressed an openness to renewing trade ties with Israel if there is progress on Israeli-Palestinian issues. In an April 2008 meeting in Qatar, Omani Foreign Affairs Minister Yusuf bin Alawi bin Abdullah informed then Israeli Foreign Minister Tzipi Livni that the Israeli trade office in Oman would remain closed until agreement was reached on a Palestinian state, although the meeting represented diplomatic outreach by Oman to Israel. There was little follow-up thereafter and Oman, like many other Arab states, considers Israeli Prime Minister Benjamin Netanyahu opposed to a settlement that would be acceptable to the Palestinians. Nevertheless, several Israeli officials reportedly visited Oman in November 2009 to attend the annual conference of the Desalination Center, and the Israeli delegation held talks with Omani officials on the margins of the conference.[19] Oman reiterated its offer to resume trade contacts with Israel if Israel agrees to at least a temporary halt in Israeli settlement construction in the West Bank. Israel has not maintained such a suspension and Israel and Oman have not reopened trade offices. Oman supports the Palestinian Authority (PA) drive for full U.N. recognition and the Omani official press refers to the PA-run territories as the "State of Palestine."

Yemen

Oman's relations with neighboring Yemen have historically been troubled, giving Oman a significant stake in political stabilization there. The former People's Democratic Republic of Yemen (PDRY), considered Marxist and pro-Soviet, supported Oman's Dhofar rebellion in the 1960s and early 1970s. Oman-PDRY relations were normalized in 1983, but the two engaged in occasional border clashes later in that decade. Relations improved after 1990, when PDRY merged with North Yemen to form the Republic of Yemen. In May 2009, Oman signaled support for Yemen's integrity and the government of President Ali Abdullah Saleh by withdrawing the Omani citizenship of southern Yemeni politician Ali Salim Al Bidh, an advocate of separatism in south Yemen.

Oman closely watched the 2011 uprising in Yemen out of concern that violence might increase and destabilize the southern Arabian peninsula. Oman built some refugee camps near its border with Yemen to accommodate refugees fleeing violence there. As part of the GCC, Oman backed the GCC efforts to negotiate a peaceful transition from the rule of Ali Abdullah Saleh, who returned to Yemen in late September 2011 following recuperation in Saudi Arabia from an attack in June 2011. Saleh agreed in December 2011 to give up power and he departed Yemen in January 2012 line with the GCC plan. However, stability has not fully returned, and Al Qaedalinked groups have reportedly taken advantage of the turmoil to increase their influence in parts of Yemen. According to the State Department FY2013 foreign aid budget justification, this has caused Oman to redeploy assets to better secure its border with Yemen, in the process thinning out Oman's capabilities elsewhere. In July 2013, Oman arrested nine Omanis for an alleged role in smuggling arms through Oman and reportedly bound for Yemen.

Other GCC and Regional Issues: Bahrain, Libya, and Syria

Oman, as do the other GCC states, fully backs the Al Khalifa regime in Bahrain in its confrontation with mostly Shiite opposition protests. Oman supported the GCC consensus to send forces from the GCC joint "Peninsula Shield" unit into Bahrain on March 14, 2011, to provide backing to the regime's beleaguered security forces, although Omani did not include any of its forces in that deployment. The GCC forces were withdrawn in June 2011.The GCC countries also decided, in March 2011, to set up a $20 billion fund to help the two members, Bahrain and Oman, that were facing popular unrest, to be used to create jobs and take other steps to ease protester anger.

Oman: Reform, Security, and U.S. Policy 25

In order to ensure that Shiite factions do not take power in Bahrain, at a GCC leadership meeting on May 14, 2012, Saudi Arabia advanced a plan for political unity among the GCC states. A unity agreement would presumably give Saudi Arabia greater justification to intervene again in Bahrain on the Bahrain royal family's behalf. However, the plan was not adopted due to concerns among the other GCC leaders about surrendering some of their sovereignty. Observers say that Oman was among the most vociferous opponents of the Saudi plan.[20]

Oman did not appear to have played as active a role in supporting the Libya uprising as its fellow GCC states Qatar and UAE. According to a wide range of accounts, Oman did not supply weapons or advice to rebel forces. Oman recognized the opposition Transitional National Council as the legitimate government of Libya only after Tripoli fell to the rebellion on August 21, 2011. In late March 2013, Oman granted asylum to the widow of slain, ousted Libyan leader Muammar Qadhafi and his daughter, Aisha, and sons Mohammad and Hannibal.[21] They reportedly had entered Oman in October 2012. Aisha and Hannibal are wanted by Interpol pursuant to a request from the Libyan government, but Libya has not asked for their extradition. Omani officials said they were granted asylum on the grounds that they not engage in any political activities.

Oman is part of the Arab League. It backed an Arab League plan to try to broker a resolution of the unrest in Syria, including the December 2011 deployment of Arab League monitors that would facilitate a withdrawal of the Syrian military from civilian neighborhoods. In November 2011, Oman voted to suspend Syria's membership in the Arab League. In 2012, in concert with the other GCC states, Oman closed its embassy in Damascus. Some GCC states, including Saudi Arabia and Qatar, are widely reported to be arming Syria's opposition, but Oman apparently is providing neither funds nor arms to armed groups in Syria. The GCC has recognized the reorganized Syrian opposition political umbrella formed in early November 2012 as the sole representative of the Syrian people, and it has decided to expel Hezbollah sympathizers from the GCC states because of Hezbollah's fighting on the side government side of the Syria conflict.

Border Disputes with UAE

Border disputes and political differences between Oman and the United Arab Emirates (UAE) have sometimes flared. The two countries finalized their borders only in 2008, nearly a decade after a tentative border settlement in 1999. In January 2011, Oman arrested several UAE citizens that it said were spying on Oman. That came a few months after the UAE arrested about 25 Omanis on similar accusations. Some observers believe the two may indeed be spying on each other because of their differing views on Iran; the UAE is more suspicious of Iran than is Oman.

ECONOMIC AND TRADE ISSUES[22]

Despite Omani efforts to diversify its economy, oil exports generate about 60% of government revenues. Oman has a relatively small 5.5 billion barrels (maximum estimate) of proven oil reserves, enough for about 15 years, and some energy development firms say that production at some Omani fields is declining.[23] Recognizing its future budgetary limitations, the government is attempting to address a perception in the public that encourages public sector employment. In a November 12, 2012, speech to open the fall session of the Oman Council, Sultan Qaboos said "The state, with all its civil, security, and military institutions, cannot continue to be the main source of employment.... The citizens have to understand that the private sector is the real source of employment in the long run."

The United States is Oman's fourth-largest trading partner, and there was over $3 billion in bilateral trade in 2012, nearly double the $1.87 billion in 2010 but down about $500 million from 2011. In 2012, the United States exported $1.747 billion in goods to Oman, and imported $1.354 billion in goods from Oman. Of U.S. exports to Oman, the largest product categories are automobiles, aircraft (including military) and related parts, drilling and other oilfield equipment, and other machinery. Of the imports, about 60% of the 2012 total consisted of fertilizers/pesticides and crude oil.

Oman is not a member of the Organization of the Petroleum Exporting Countries (OPEC) and is therefore not bound by an oil export quota set by that organization. Recognizing that its crude oil fields are aging, Oman is trying to privatize its economy, diversify its sources of revenue, and develop its liquid natural gas (LNG) sector, for which Oman has identified large markets in Asia and elsewhere. Gas ventures with Iran that are under discussion were addressed above, in the "Iran" section. In November 2008, Oman signed a 20-year agreement with Occidental Petroleum to develop existing gas fields and explore for new ones. Oman is part of the "Dolphin project," under which Qatar is exporting natural gas to UAE and Oman through undersea pipelines; it began operations in 2007. The natural gas supplies to Oman from Dolphin free up other Omani natural gas supplies for sale to its customers. The need to

Oman: Reform, Security, and U.S. Policy

diversify may have gained further urgency in August 2011 when Reliance Energy Ltd. of India abandoned plans to develop an offshore oil block six years after signing a production sharing agreement with the government.

Oman was admitted to the WTO in September 2000. The U.S.-Oman Free Trade Agreement was signed on January 19, 2006, and ratified by Congress (P.L. 109-283, signed September 26, 2006). According to the U.S. embassy in Muscat, the FTA has led to increased partnerships between Omani and U.S. companies. General Cables and Dura-Line Middle East are two successful examples of joint ventures between American and Omani firms. Notably, these two new ventures are not focused on hydrocarbons, which serves to show that the U.S.-Omani trade relationship is varied and not focused only on oil.

Economic Aid

The United States phased out development assistance to Oman in 1996. At the height of that development assistance program in the 1980s, the United States was giving Oman about $15 million per year in Economic Support Funds (ESF) in loans and grants, mostly for conservation and management of Omani fisheries and water resources.

End Notes

[1] Much of this and the subsequent section is from the State Department's country report on human rights practices for 2012 (released April 19, 2013), http://www.state the *International Religious Freedom Report* for 2012 (May 20, 2013), http://www.state.gov /j/drl/rls/irf/religiousfreedom/index.htm?year=2012&dlid=208398#wrapper; and the *Trafficking in Persons Report for 2013* (June 19, 2013), http://www.state.gov/documents /organization/210740.pdf

[2] Author conversations with Omani officials in Washington, D.C., June 2013.

[3] Author conversation with Omani Foreign Ministry consultant and unofficial envoy. May 5, 2011. This official has a name nearly identical to that of the Minister of State for Defense, but they are two different officials.

[4] http://oman.usembassy.gov/pr-06012011.html

[5] Hajjar, Sami. *U.S. Military Presence in the Gulf: Challenges and Prospects.* U.S. Army War College, Strategic Studies Institute. P. 27. The State and Defense Departments have not released public information recently on the duration of the 2010 renewal of the agreements or modifications to the agreements, if any.

[6] Finnegan, Philip. "Oman Seeks U.S. Base Upgrades." *Defense News*, April 12, 1999.

[7] Author conversation with Muscat Daily reporter about Musnanah. April 28, 2011.

[8] Author conversation with State Department officer responsible for Oman. January 6, 2011.

[9] Contingency Tracking System Deployment File, provided to CRS by the Department of Defense.

[10] Section 564 of Title V, Part C of the Foreign Relations Authorization Act for FY1994 and FY1995 (P.L. 103-236) banned U.S. arms transfers to countries that maintain the Arab boycott of Israel during those fiscal years. As applied to the GCC states, this provision was waived on the grounds that doing so was in the national interest.

[11] Andrea Shalal-Esa. "Lockheed Hopes to Finalize F-16 Sales to Iraq, Oman." Reuters, May 16, 2011.

[12] http://www.google 352110feed177d190098ee9d6.241

[13] http://www.state

[14] Dennis Hevesi. "Philo Dibble, Diplomat and Iran Expert, Dies At 60." *New York Times*, October 13, 2011.

[15] Iran, Oman Ink Agreement of Defensive Cooperation. Tehran Fars News Agency, August 4, 2010.

[16] Ibid.

[17] CRS conversations with U.S. Embassy officials in Oman. 1995-2003.

[18] "Mullen, Mattis Meet With Omani Counterparts." American Forces Press Service. February 24, 2011.

[19] Ravid, Barak. "Top Israeli Diplomat Holds Secret Talks in Oman." Haaretz, November 25, 2009. http://www.haaretz.com/hasen/spages/1130242.html

[20] Comments to the author by a visiting GCC official. May 2012.

[21] "Muammar Gaddafi's Family Granted Asylum in Oman." Reuters, March 25, 2013.

[22] For more information on Oman's economy and U.S.-Oman trade, see CRS Report RL33328, *U.S.-Oman Free Trade Agreement*, by Mary Jane Bolle.

[23] Gerth, Jeff and Stephen Labaton. "Oman's Oil Yield Long in Decline, Shell Data Show." *New York Times*, April 8, 2004.

In: Oman: Conditions, Issues and U.S. Relations   ISBN: 978-1-62948-086-2
Editor: Sebastian Haas   © 2013 Nova Science Publishers, Inc.

Chapter 2

OMAN 2012 HUMAN RIGHTS REPORT[*]

U.S. Department of State

EXECUTIVE SUMMARY

The Sultanate of Oman is ruled by a hereditary monarchy. Sultan Qaboos al-Said has ruled since 1970. The sultan has sole authority to enact laws through royal decree, although ministries draft laws and citizens provide input through the bicameral Majlis Oman (Oman Council). The Majlis is composed of the Majlis al- Dawla (State Council), whose 83 members are appointed by the sultan, and the elected, 84-member Majlis al-Shura (Consultative Council). The last elections took place on December 22 when citizens chose among 1,600 candidates to elect 192 citizens to seats in 11 municipal councils. The 29-member Council of Ministers, selected by the sultan, advises him on government decisions. In 2011 a new law granted the Oman Council powers that expanded its policy review function to include approving, rejecting, and amending legislation and convoking ministers of agencies that provide direct citizen services. Security forces report to civilian authorities.

The principal human rights problems were the inability of citizens to change their government, limits on freedom of speech and assembly, and discrimination against women, including political and economic exclusion based on cultural norms. Thirty-two individuals were convicted on charges of

---

[*] This is an edited, reformatted and augmented version of the U.S. Department of State; Bureau of Democracy, Human Rights and Labor, dated May, 2013.

libel against the sultan during the year, receiving prison sentences from six to 18 months and fines of 500 to 1,000 Omani rials (approximately $1,300 to $2,600). Another 12 individuals were convicted on charges of illegal assembly (assembly without a permit) while peacefully protesting some of the libel convictions. The protesters each received a prison sentence of one year and a 1,000 rial fine (approximately $2,600).

Other ongoing concerns included lack of independent inspections of prisons and detention centers, restrictions on press freedom, instances of domestic violence, and instances of foreign citizen laborers placed in conditions of forced labor or abuse.

Security personnel and other government officials generally were held accountable for their actions. The Head of Finance of the Royal Oman Police (ROP) was prosecuted, sentenced, and jailed for four-and-a-half years for embezzlement of over 700,000 Omani rials (approximately $1.8 million). In a separate case, after security forces shot and killed a protester in 2011, authorities conducted an investigation but held no one liable.

SECTION 1. RESPECT FOR THE INTEGRITY OF THE PERSON, INCLUDING FREEDOM FROM

a. Arbitrary or Unlawful Deprivation of Life

During the year there were no reports of protesters being killed or other arbitrary or unlawful killings. In contrast, throughout 2011 there were reports that security forces shot and killed up to six protesters while dispersing protests and demonstrations. The Ministry of Health reported that only one protester died during the demonstrations.

In April, 23 persons received prison terms ranging from a few months to five years for their participation in a February 2011 protest where security forces killed one individual.

b. Disappearance

Politically motivated disappearances were reported in the country. On May 31, security forces detained Ismael al-Meqbali, Habiba al-Hinai, and Yaqoub al- Kharusi, human rights activists who were visiting striking oil workers. Authorities released al-Hinai and charged al-Kharusi. Al-Meqbali's friends and family were not informed of his whereabouts for weeks. Eventually, authorities permitted al- Meqbali to speak to his family by telephone and allowed his brother to visit him in detention.

In 2011 human rights activists, Saeed al-Hashmi and Basma al-Rajhi, reported being abducted from their car by several men, taken to a remote area, and beaten. Al-Hashmi and al-Rajhi alleged that their kidnappers demanded they stop their political activities. Although they reported the incident to police, authorities have not identified the attackers.

c. Torture and Other Cruel, Inhuman, or Degrading Treatment or Punishment

While the law prohibits such practices, prisoners detained on charges of seditious assembly complained of sleep deprivation, subjection to extremely cold temperatures, and solitary confinement. The government denied these accusations, made no investigation into the complaints, and did not charge any officers.

On October 19, human rights activist Basma al-Rajhi reported that authorities kept her in a police-run hospital for several days following her attack in the desert a year earlier. While she was at the hospital, al-Rajhi claimed a security services officer accompanied her at all times and that medical personnel conducted a virginity test on her.

Prison and Detention Center Conditions
Prison and detention center conditions generally met international standards; however, there were reports that security forces abused prisoners held on politically sensitive charges.

Physical Conditions: Prisoners had access to potable water. Conditions for female prisoners were on par with those of their male counterparts. Political prisoners reported experiencing worse treatment than individuals charged with criminal offenses. The primary detention center for illegal immigrants was overcrowded. There were on average 750 convicted individuals in jail during the year and another few hundred awaiting trial. There were also several hundred undocumented immigrants in detention centers awaiting deportation.

On June 11, authorities arrested two women along with 20 other protesters. Authorities held them under administrative detention without

32 U.S. Department of State

charge or trial and denied access to family, friends, and their lawyers for several days. The two women, Basma al-Kiyumi and Basima al-Rajhi, reported they did not receive any access to medical treatment. The two reportedly were on a hunger strike for seven days.

In December 2011 several detainees convicted of crimes related to illegal protesting began a hunger strike that lasted approximately one week. Those detained on charges of illegal assembly complained of poor medical treatment, including treatment by other prisoners instead of by professional medical personnel.

Administration: There were no complaints about poor recordkeeping in the prison system, and consequently the government did not take any steps to improve it. Alternative sentencing for nonviolent prisoners was not available. There is no ombudsman to serve on behalf of prisoners and detainees. Prisoners and detainees did not always have reasonable access to visitors, as in the case of Ismael al- Meqbali. Authorities permitted prisoners to have religious observance. Authorities allowed prisoners and detainees to submit complaints to judicial authorities without censorship and to request investigation of credible allegations of inhumane conditions. The National Human Rights Commission (NHRC), a governmental body, investigated and monitored prison and detention center conditions through site visits, and authorities in some cases investigated claims of abuse, but the results of investigations were not documented in a publicly accessible manner.

Monitoring: The law permitted visits by independent human rights observers; however, there were no actual independent human rights observer groups working in the country. Consular services from various embassies and the NHRC regularly visited prisons and met with prisoners.

d. Arbitrary Arrest or Detention

The law prohibits arbitrary arrest and detention, and the government generally observed these prohibitions. There was one report of a foreign citizen woman held in a women's prison for 18 months without charge; the NHRC also investigated and resolved the case. Following the release of several individuals on bail accused of illegal assembly, security forces rearrested several of the defendants on unknown charges.

Role of the Police and Security Apparatus

The Royal Office, part of the cabinet, controls internal and external security and coordinates all intelligence and security policies. Under the Royal Office, the Internal Security Service investigates all matters related to domestic security, and the sultan's Special Forces have limited border security and antismuggling responsibilities. The ROP, also part of the cabinet, perform regular police duties, provide security at points of entry, serve as the country's immigration and customs agency, and includes the Coast Guard. The Ministry of Defense, and in particular the Royal Army of Oman (RAO), is responsible for securing the borders and has limited domestic security responsibilities. The security forces performed their duties effectively.

Civilian authorities generally maintained effective control over the Internal Security Service, the sultan's Special Forces, the RAO, and the ROP.

Arrest Procedures and Treatment While in Detention

The law does not require police to obtain a warrant before making an arrest but provides that police must either release the person or refer the matter to the public prosecutor within specified time frames. For most crimes, the public prosecutor must formally arrest or release the person within 48 hours of detention; however, the law permits authorities to hold individuals for up to 30 days without charge in cases related to security. There was a functioning bail system for most individuals, but some prisoners granted bail and released by civilian judges were immediately rearrested by security forces. Detainees generally had prompt access to a lawyer of their choice, although meetings between some prisoners and their attorneys were allowed only in the presence of the public prosecutor. At least one detainee, al- Meqbali, reportedly did not have access to an attorney for at least two weeks after his initial detention. The state provided public attorneys to indigent detainees. Authorities generally allowed detainees prompt access to family members, but police sometimes failed to notify a detainee's family, as in al-Meqbali's case. In cases involving foreign citizen workers, police sometimes failed to notify the detainee's local sponsor.

Arbitrary Arrest: The law prohibits arbitrary arrest and detention, but it reportedly occurred in cases relating to political protests.

Pretrial Detention: For crimes related to terrorism or national security, the law allows police to hold a detainee for up to 30 days without charge, and authorities used this law several times during the year. Court orders are

34 U.S. Department of State

required to hold suspects in pretrial detention. Judges may order detentions for 14 days to allow investigation and may grant extensions at their discretion. In most cases, judges permitted defendants to be released on bail while lengthy investigations took place.

Amnesty: The sultan tended to pardon and grant amnesties to prisoners throughout the year and on holidays. On July 23, the sultan pardoned 182 prisoners including 86 foreigners. The sultan pardoned 278 prisoners for Eid al-Adha, 215 prisoners for Eid al-Fitr, and 115 prisoners for National Day. The pardons were for petty criminals and not for prisoners on charges related to security or freedom of expression.

e. Denial of Fair Public Trial

Although the law provides for an independent judiciary, the sultan may act as a court of final appeal and exercise his power of pardon as chairman of the Supreme Judicial Council, the country's highest legal body, which is empowered to review all judicial decisions. Authorities generally respected court orders; however, a number of individuals who were released from detention were immediately rearrested on unknown charges. While the government generally respected judicial independence, in the case of some defendants held on charges of illegal assembly, there were reports that the government improperly influenced judges in their cases. In 2011 the media questioned government influence in the *Azzaman* newspaper case, in which two of the newspaper's editors and one government employee were convicted of slander. Principles of Sharia (Islamic law) inform the civil, commercial, and criminal codes. There were no women judges. Civilian or military courts try all cases.

Trial Procedures

The law provides for the right to a fair trial and stipulates the presumption of innocence. Language interpretation for non-Arabic speakers was frequently unavailable. Citizens and legally resident noncitizens have the right to a public trial, except when the court decides to hold a session in private in the interest of public order or morals, and the judiciary generally enforced this right. While the vast majority of legal proceedings were open to the public, lese-majeste and freedom of expression trials were sometimes closed. There is no trial by jury.

Defendants have the right to be present, consult with an attorney in a timely manner, present evidence, and confront witnesses. Courts provide public attorneys to indigent detainees and offer legal defense for defendants facing prison terms of three years or more. The prosecution and defense counsel direct questions to witnesses through the judge. Defendants and their lawyers generally had access to government-held evidence relevant to their cases. Those convicted in any court have one opportunity to appeal a jail sentence longer than three months and fines of more than 480 rials (approximately $1,250) to the appellate and supreme courts. The judiciary generally enforced these rights for all citizens. In contravention to the law, however, some judges in provincial areas occasionally discriminated against female defendants by requesting that they appear in court with their fathers or husbands. In such cases women could seek redress for such treatment by appealing through the courts.

Political Prisoners and Detainees

The courts convicted 32 individuals for peaceful activities, including posting comments on social media Web sites and participating in peaceful demonstrations in which they either directly or indirectly criticized the government. They received prison sentences of six to 18 months and fines of 200 to 1,000 rials (approximately $520 to $2,600). For example, in late May and early June, authorities arrested Ishaq al-Aghbari, Ismael al-Meqbali, Ali al-Haji, Mahmoud al-Jamoudi, Hassan al- Rauqaishi, Nabhan al-Hanashi, Khaled al-Noufali, Sultan al-Sa'adi, and Hatim al-Maliki for offenses including insulting the sultan, undermining the status of the state, and using the Internet to publish defamatory material. On June 11, police arrested over 20 human rights activists in front of a police station in Muscat for demanding the release of the activists who had recently been detained. Political prisoners reported that they received worse treatment than other prisoners.

Civil Judicial Procedures and Remedies

Civil laws govern civil cases. Citizens and nonnationals were able to file cases, including lawsuits seeking damages for human rights violations. The judiciary was generally independent and impartial, and police enforced court orders effectively for all persons. The Administrative Court reviews complaints about the misuse of governmental authority. It has the power to reverse decisions by government bodies and to award compensation. Appointments to this court are subject to the approval of the Administrative Affairs Council. The court's president and deputy president are appointed by

36 U.S. Department of State

royal decree based on the council's nomination. Citizens and foreign workers may file complaints regarding working conditions with the Ministry of Manpower for alternative dispute resolution. The ministry may refer cases to the courts if it is unable to negotiate a solution.

f. Arbitrary Interference with Privacy, Family, Home, or Correspondence

The law does not require police to obtain search warrants before entering homes, but they often obtained warrants from the Public Prosecutor's Office. The government monitored private communications, including cell phone, e-mail, and Internet chat room exchanges.

The Ministry of Interior required citizens to obtain permission to marry foreigners, except nationals of Gulf Cooperation Council (GCC) countries, whom citizens may marry without restriction; permission was not automatically granted. Citizen marriage to a foreigner abroad without ministry approval may result in denial of entry for the foreign spouse at the border and preclude children from claiming citizenship rights. It also may result in a bar from government employment and a 2,000 rial fine (approximately $5,200).

SECTION 2. RESPECT FOR CIVIL LIBERTIES, INCLUDING

a. Freedom of Speech and Press

The law provides for limited freedom of speech and press. However, in practice authorities did not respect these rights during the year. Journalists and writers exercised self-censorship.

Freedom of Speech: The law prohibits criticism of the sultan in any form or medium; "material that leads to public discord, violates the security of the state, or abuses a person's dignity or his rights"; "messages of any form that violate public order and morals or are harmful to a person's safety"; and "defamation of character." Therefore, it is illegal to insult any public official, and individuals sometimes were prosecuted for doing so. Thirty-two individuals received prison sentences for directly or indirectly criticizing the sultan in online fora and at peaceful protests. For example, on July 16, the Muscat Court of First Instance convicted six individuals of "defaming the sultan." The court sentenced each to one year in prison and a 1,000 rial ($2,600) fine. Three of these individuals, Mona Hardan, Talib al-Abry, and Mohammed al-Badi, received an additional six-month sentence for violating the cyber crimes law. According to reports, the convictions were the result of Facebook postings and Twitter comments deemed critical of the sultan. On July 9, the Muscat Court of First Instance convicted four other individuals with "defaming the sultan." These individuals were reportedly convicted for carrying signs critical of the sultan at demonstrations.

Freedom of Press: The media generally does not operate freely. Authorities tolerated limited criticism regarding domestic and foreign affairs in privately owned newspapers and magazines, although editorials generally were consistent with the government's views. The government and privately owned radio and television stations did not generally broadcast political material. There was no permanent international media presence in the country.

Violence and Harassment: There were isolated instances where authorities harassed journalists during the year. On January 15, GulfNews.com reported that authorities detained and questioned two Indian journalists with the *Muscat Daily* who were trying to interview and photograph striking workers. According to reports, the striking workers mobbed the journalists to get their grievances published. After management representatives asked the journalists to leave, plainclothes police officers detained them outside of the work camp and brought them to the Seeb Police Station. The journalists reported that authorities interrogated them extensively before releasing them without charge.

Censorship or Content Restrictions: Headlines in both public and private media print outlets were subject to an official, nontransparent review and approval process before publication. Journalists and writers exercised self-censorship. For example, one media outlet chose not to report that the government was likely inflating the voter turnout figures during the year's municipal council elections, for fear of contradicting the Ministry of Interior's official announcement.

Libel Laws/National Security: The government used libel laws and national security concerns as grounds to suppress criticism of government figures and politically objectionable views. Libel was a criminal offense, and the government strictly enforced laws with heavy fines and prison sentences.

38   U.S. Department of State

The government also prohibited publication of any material that "violated the security of the state." On one occasion government-owned newspapers published photographs and biographic data of individuals convicted of insulting the sultan, contrary to normal practice where convicts' faces are obscured in newspaper articles. The newspapers apologized after public outcry but later republished the pictures.

In 2011 a court sentenced *Azzaman* journalist Ibrahim al-Ma'mari, editor in chief Yusuf al-Haj, and Ministry of Justice employee Haroon al-Muqaibli to five months in prison for crimes relating to accusations against the minister of justice published in the *Azzaman* newspaper. Al-Muqaibli won the case on appeal. The case was resolved with a one-month temporary closure of the paper and a full-page apology printed in the paper when it reopened.

On February 7, security services detained activist Muawiya al-Rawahy after he published a blog entry criticizing the overall situation in the country and expressing a lack of confidence in the reign of Sultan Qaboos. The blog entry was deleted following his initial detention, and courts sentenced al-Rawahy to one year in prison and a fine of 200 rials ($520).

Publishing Restrictions: The law permits the Ministry of Information to review all media products and books produced within or imported into the country. The ministry occasionally prohibited or censored material from domestic and imported publications viewed as politically, culturally, or sexually offensive. Some books were not permitted in the country. There were no major publishing houses in the country, and publication of books remained limited.

Internet Freedom

The law restricts free speech via the Internet, and the government enforced the restrictions. The government's national telecommunications company and private service providers made Internet access available for a fee to citizens and foreign residents. Internet access was available via schools, workplaces, wide area networks at coffee shops, and other venues, especially in urban areas.

Authorities monitored the activities of telecommunications service providers and obliged them to block access to numerous Web sites considered pornographic, culturally or politically sensitive, or competitive with local telecommunications services. The criteria for blocking access to Internet sites were not transparent or consistent. Web blogs were sometimes blocked. All video-chat technologies, such as Skype, are illegal. Authorities also blocked

Oman 2012 Human Rights Report   39

some Web sites used to circumvent censorship, such as virtual private networks.

The law details crimes that take place on the Internet, which "might prejudice public order or religious values" and specifies a penalty of between one month and a year in prison and fines of not less than 1,000 rials (approximately $2,600). Authorities have also applied the law against bloggers and social media users who break lese-majeste laws.

Authorities charged and convicted at least eight activists under the Cyber Crime law. These individuals, including Ali al-Haji and Nabhan al-Hanashi, received prison sentences of six months (18 months when combined with charges of slandering the sultan) and fines of 1,000 riyals ($2,600.)

The government placed warnings on Web sites informing users that criticism of the sultan or personal criticism of government officials would be censored and could lead to police questioning, effectively increasing self-censorship. The public prosecutor's office sent out text messages reminding persons of defamation laws.

Web site administrators or moderators were cautious concerning content and were reportedly quick to delete potentially offensive material in chat rooms, on social networking fora, and on blog postings.

Academic Freedom and Cultural Events

The government limited academic freedom, particularly the publication or discussion of controversial matters such as domestic politics, through the threat of dismissal. Academics largely practiced self-censorship. On August 8, press reported that authorities banned an Indian film that contained sexually explicit dialogue.

The government censored publicly shown films, primarily for sexual content and nudity.

b. Freedom of Peaceful Assembly and Association

Freedom of Assembly

The law provides for limited freedom of assembly and the government restricted this right in practice. Government approval was necessary for all public gatherings with over nine persons present, although there was no clear process for obtaining approval for public demonstrations. Authorities enforced this requirement sporadically. Individuals who were detained for participating

40   U.S. Department of State

in illegal gatherings and unauthorized protests occasionally reported that arresting officers insulted them.

In April 2011 a protest in Sohar resulted in the death of one man at the hands of security forces. Five hundred protesters were assembled to protest for economic and government reforms. Ultimately, 23 persons were convicted of violent behavior and illegal weapons possession and received prison terms ranging from a few months to five years (see section 1.a.).

On April 5, reports indicated that Jordanian authorities told Ammar al-Ma'amari, an Omani student studying law in Jordan, to prepare for deportation to Oman. Al- Ma'amari's blog reportedly came to the attention of Omani authorities due to posts covering the security services during the suppression of protests in 2011 and published medical reports for Abdullah Ghamlasa, the protester killed in February 2011. At year's end al-Ma'amari had not been deported. On June 11, in a separate case, police detained 30 protesters for an illegal protest outside the office of the Public Prosecution in support of those arrested on lese-majeste charges. The detained protesters were initially held at Sumail Central Prison and formally charged with inciting or taking part in protests. One of the protesters, Saeed al- Hashmi, reportedly went on a hunger strike to protest the group's detention. He was admitted to Sumail Hospital on June 14 after he reportedly lost consciousness. He later recovered. Reports indicated some of the female protesters started to refuse water to protest their detention but then were formally charged and released. Their health was reportedly not in danger. Twelve were eventually charged and convicted of illegal assembly; they were sentenced to one year in prison and a 1,000 rial fine (approximately $2,600).

Freedom of Association

The law provides for freedom of association "for legitimate objectives and in a proper manner." The law does not clearly define "legitimate objective." Examples of associations include labor unions. The council of ministers limited freedom of association in practice by prohibiting associations whose activities were deemed "inimical to the social order" or otherwise not appropriate, and did not license groups regarded as a threat to the predominant social and political views or the interests of the country. Associations also must register with the Ministry of Social Development, which approves all associations' bylaws. The average time required to register an association ranged from two months to two years. Approval time varied based on the level of preparedness of the applying organization and the subject matter of the organization, as well its leadership. It was often longer when a group required

Oman 2012 Human Rights Report 41

significant help from the ministry to formalize its structure. Formal registration of nationality-based associations was limited to one association for each nationality.

No association may receive funding from an international group without government approval. Individuals convicted of doing so for an association may receive up to six months in jail and a fine of 500 rials (approximately $1,300). Heads of domestic NGOs reported that the government periodically asked to review their financial records to confirm sources of funding and required NGOs to inform the government of any meetings with foreign organizations or diplomatic missions.

c. Freedom of Religion

See the Department of State's *International Religious Freedom Report* at www.state.

d. Freedom of Movement, Internally Displaced Persons, Protection of Refugees, and Stateless Persons

The law provides for freedom of movement within the country and repatriation, and the government generally respected these rights in practice. The law does not specifically provide for foreign travel or emigration. The Office of the UN High Commissioner for Refugees (UNHCR) did not visit the country during the year, and it did not maintain an office or personnel in the country. Some humanitarian organizations were restricted in their ability to provide refugees with assistance. Specifically, authorities prohibited UNICEF from fulfilling the UNHCR's role in its absence, although the government allowed other entities, such as the Oman Charitable Organization, to assist refugees.

In-country Movement: There were no official government restrictions on internal travel for any citizen. However, the government must approve travel by foreign diplomats to Dhofar and Musandam regions. Foreigners could not change jobs without obtaining sponsorship from the new employer.

Foreign Travel: Foreigners must obtain an exit visa from their employer prior to leaving the country. Exit visas may be denied when there is a dispute

42 U.S. Department of State

over payment or work remaining, leaving the foreign citizen in country without recourse besides local courts.

Protection of Refugees

Access to Asylum: The laws provide for the granting of asylum or refugee status, and the government has established a system for providing protection to refugees. The ROP is responsible for determining refugee status but did not grant asylum or accept refugees for resettlement during the year. The ROP's system for granting refugee status is not transparent, and the law does not specify a time frame in which the ROP must adjudicate an asylum application.

Refoulement: In practice the government did not provide protection against the return of refugees to countries where their lives or freedom would be threatened. Tight control over the entry of foreigners effectively limited access to protection for refugees and asylum seekers. Authorities apprehended and deported hundreds of presumed economic migrants from Somalia, Yemen, Ethiopia, and Eritrea who sought to enter the country illegally by land and sea in the south, and Afghans and Pakistanis who generally came to the country by boat via Iran. Authorities generally detained these persons in centers in Salalah or the northern port city of Sohar, where they were detained an average of one month before deportation to their countries of origin.

Access to Basic Services: Without an official sponsor, it is difficult for economic migrants to have access to basic services. Many applied to their embassies for repatriation.

Temporary Protection: Embassies and ethnic or language community welfare groups provided temporary protections. The government did not provide temporary protection to individuals who qualify as refugees.

SECTION 3. RESPECT FOR POLITICAL RIGHTS: THE RIGHT OF CITIZENS TO CHANGE THEIR GOVERNMENT

The law does not provide citizens with the right to change their government. The sultan retains ultimate authority on all foreign and domestic issues. With the exception of the military and other security forces, all citizens 21 years old and older have the right to vote for candidates for the

Consultative Council and the provincial councils. In 2011 the sultan issued a royal decree granting limited legislative authority to the Consultative Council, which can either approve or suggest amendments to new laws. On December 22, citizens elected municipal councils to advise the Royal Court on the service needs of their communities.

Elections and Political Participation

Recent Elections: On December 22, approximately 546,000 citizens participated in elections for provincial councils. Of the more than 1,600 candidates running for 192 seats, 48 were women. In October 2011 approximately 60 percent of 518,000 registered voters participated in elections for the Consultative Council. Electoral commissions review potential candidates against a set of objective educational and character criteria (high school education, no criminal history, or mental illness) before allowing candidates' names on the ballot. The Ministry of Interior closely monitored campaign materials and events in its role as the ministry in charge of elections. There were no notable or widespread allegations of fraud or improper government interference in the voting process. The government did not allow independent monitoring of the elections.

Political Parties: The law does not allow political parties, and citizens did not attempt to form any.

Participation of Women and Minorities: Women were largely excluded from senior decision-making positions and were prevented from participating equally in political life due to conservative social constraints. During the December 22 elections, voters elected four women as representatives on provincial councils. Forty-eight women ran among an estimated 1,600 candidates for 192 representative spots across 11 provincial councils. The government has taken steps to address this situation; the sultan appointed 15 women to the 93-member State Council and two women, the ministers of education and of higher education, to the 29-member Council of Ministers.

SECTION 4. CORRUPTION AND LACK OF TRANSPARENCY IN GOVERNMENT

The law provides criminal penalties for official corruption, and the government generally implemented these laws effectively. There were isolated reports of government corruption during the year, including in the police and other security organizations. Public officials are subject to financial disclosure laws. When selected for disclosure, officials are required to list their finances, business interests, and property, as well as that of their spouses and children. While these records will be made public, there are no sanctions for noncompliance.

On August 17, a court convicted a high-ranking member of the ROP of accepting bribes and misappropriating public funds. The court sentenced him to three years in prison and ordered him to pay a fine of more than 90,000 rials (approximately $234,000). The media published his name and photograph in the local press. In September 2011 a court convicted and sentenced two mid-level officials at the Ministry of Environment and Climate Affairs to prison for their role in the "stone-crushing" case. In October 2011 the undersecretary for justice was replaced following reports of misuse of power.

The law does not provide for public access to government information, although all royal decrees and ministerial decisions were published.

SECTION 5. GOVERNMENTAL ATTITUDE REGARDING INTERNATIONAL AND NONGOVERNMENTAL INVESTIGATION OF ALLEGED VIOLATIONS OF HUMAN RIGHTS

No registered or fully autonomous domestic human rights organizations existed. There were civil society groups that advocated for persons protected under human rights conventions, particularly women and the disabled. These groups were required to register with the Ministry of Social Development.

The government did not support international or domestic human rights organizations operating in the country.

UN and Other International Bodies: The government allowed some international organizations to work in the country without interference on a nonresident basis, including the World Health Organization, and the

Oman 2012 Human Rights Report

International Labor Organization. The UNICEF and the UN Population Fund both have resident offices in the country.

Government Human Rights Bodies: The NHRC, a government-funded commission made up of members from the public, private, and academic sectors, reported on human rights to the sultan via the State Council. During the year the commission issued its first human rights report, which it submitted to the UN Human Rights Council, and is available publically on their Web site. It continued investigating 169 human rights complaints it had received during the year. The NHRC also conducted prison visits and continued a community and school outreach program to discuss human rights with students.

SECTION 6. DISCRIMINATION, SOCIETAL ABUSES, AND TRAFFICKING IN PERSONS

The law prohibits discrimination against citizens on the basis of gender, ethnic origin, race, language, religion, place of residence, and social class. The government selectively enforced prohibitions on most bases of discrimination, but did not do so for discrimination against women.

Women

Rape and Domestic Violence: The law criminalizes rape with penalties of up to 15 years in prison, but does not criminalize spousal rape. The government generally enforced the law when individuals reported cases, but reports indicated that many victims did not report rape due to cultural and societal factors.

As a result there was no reliable estimate of the extent of the problem. In 2010, the most recent year for which statistics are available, the police charged 227 individuals with rape or attempted rape. Foreign nationals working as domestic employees occasionally reported that their sponsors or employees of labor recruitment agencies had raped them. According to diplomatic observers, police investigations resulted in few rape convictions, and sponsors repatriated most of the women who made the allegations.

46 U.S. Department of State

The law does not specifically address domestic violence. Assault, battery, and aggravated assault carry a maximum sentence of three years in prison. Allegations of spousal abuse in civil courts handling family law cases reportedly were common. Victims of domestic violence may file a complaint with police. Due to societal customs, women often sought private family intervention to protect them from violent domestic situations.

Harmful Traditional Practices: There were no reports of honor killings; however, a number of women were reportedly subject to mistreatment due to behavior deemed "inappropriate."

Female Genital Mutilation/Cutting (FGM/C): Although the government prohibits female genital mutilation/cutting (FGM/C) in public hospitals and clinics, there is no law prohibiting private practitioners from performing the procedure. According to press reports, a 2010 Ministry of Health study on FGM/C found that men and women across all ages broadly accepted the practice, especially in rural areas, where it was reported to be a common occurrence. The World Health Organization lists Oman as a country of occurrence but it does not have statistics.

Sexual Harassment: The law does not specifically prohibit sexual harassment.

Reproductive Rights: The government recognized the basic right of married couples to decide freely and responsibly the number, spacing, and timing of their children. Health clinics operated freely in disseminating information on family planning under the guidance of the Ministry of Health. There were no legal restrictions on the right to access contraceptives for nonmarried individuals permitting unmarried persons to acquire birth control easily. The government provided free childbirth services to citizens within the framework of universal health care. Prenatal and postnatal care was readily available and used. Men and women received equal access to diagnosis and treatment for sexually transmitted infections, including HIV/AIDS; however, social taboos prevented individuals from seeking treatment.

Discrimination: The law prohibits gender-based discrimination against citizens. However, economic studies conducted by the World Economic Forum showed that women earned 75 percent less than men and that their unemployment rate was at least twice as high. Aspects of Islamic law and tradition as interpreted in the country discriminated against women, as did some social and legal institutions. In some personal status cases, such as divorce, a women's testimony is equal to half of a man's. The law favors male heirs in adjudicating inheritance. Women married to noncitizens may not transmit citizenship to their children and cannot sponsor their noncitizen husband's presence in the country.

The law provides citizenship at birth if the father is a citizen, if the mother is a citizen and the father is unknown, or if a child of unknown parents is found in the country. The law provides that an adult may become a citizen by applying for citizenship and subsequently residing legally in the country for 20 years or 10 years if married to a male citizen. During that time an applicant cannot reside more than one month of each year outside the country. A person seeking naturalization is expected first to give up any previous citizenship.

Women were not allowed to transmit citizenship to their spouses or children. Observers reported a few isolated cases of children without documentation as the result of a marriage between an Omani woman and a non-Omani man. These children were not eligible for citizenship.

Women may own property, but it is unknown what percentage of women actually own property. The law equalizes the treatment of men and women in receiving free government land for housing. Women may, and do, own land.

Government policy provided women with equal opportunities for education, and this policy effectively eliminated the previous gender gap in education attainment. Although some educated women held positions of authority in government, business, and the media, many women faced job discrimination based on cultural norms. The law entitles women to gender-related protections in the workplace such as the right to paid maternity leave and equal pay for equal work. The government, the largest employer of women, observed such regulations, as did many private sector employers. According to the World Economic Forum, only 27 percent of women participated in the work force.

The Ministry of Social Development is the umbrella ministry for women's affairs. The ministry provided support for women's economic development through the Oman Women's Associations and local community development centers. The government also formed a committee to monitor the country's compliance with the UN Convention on the Elimination of All Forms of Discrimination against Women.

Children

Birth Registration: Citizenship is derived from the father. Women married to noncitizens may not transmit citizenship to their children, and there were a few reported cases of stateless children based on this law. The government announced that children of unknown parents would be eligible for citizenship in 2011. Abandoned children were raised by government employees in an orphanage, given free education through the university level, and guaranteed a job following graduation, which is followed through in practice. Citizen marriage to a foreigner abroad without ministry approval may preclude children from claiming citizenship rights (see section 1.f.).

Education: Primary school education for citizen children was free and universal, but not compulsory.

Medical Care: Authorities provide free medical care to citizens.

Child Abuse: According to a domestic media report citing the Ministry of Health, approximately 20 cases of sexual abuse against children are recorded a year. The report also noted that sexual abuse most commonly involved children of both sexes between the age of six to 12 years old and was committed by close relatives or friends of the family. There was a heavy social stigma with reporting child abuse.

Child Marriage: The age of legal marriage for men and women is 18 years old, although a judge may permit a person to marry younger when the marriage is in the person's interest. According to the Organization for Economic Cooperation and Development, child marriage continues to be practiced in the country, especially in rural areas, where as many as 4 percent of girls between the ages of 15 and 19 were married.

Harmful Traditional Practices: Although the government prohibits female genital mutilation/cutting (FGM/C) in public hospitals and clinics, there is no law prohibiting private practitioners from performing the procedure. According to press reports, a 2010 Ministry of Health study on FGM/C found that men and women across all ages broadly accepted the practice, especially in rural areas, where it was reported to be a common occurrence. In the southern Dhofar region, FGM/C is performed on newborns and involves a partial or total clitoridectomy (Type I as defined by the World Health

Organization). Throughout the rest of the country, FGM/C usually consists of a minor cut made on the clitoris (Type IV). According to a newspaper report, the practice was usually carried out by persons with no medical training and in unhygienic conditions.

Sexual Exploitation of Children: Commercial sexual exploitation of children and child pornography are punishable by no less than five years' imprisonment. All sex outside of marriage was illegal, but sex with a minor under 15 years old carried a heavier penalty (up to 15 years' imprisonment). Minors are not charged. The country is not a destination for child sex tourism, and child prostitution is rare.

Institutionalized Children: Children in orphanages are generally children born out of wedlock and abandoned in hospitals at birth. While these children face social challenges, they are given free secondary education and jobs from the government.

International Child Abductions: Oman is not a party to the 1980 Hague Convention on the Civil Aspects of International Child Abduction.

Anti-Semitism

There was no local Jewish population, and there were no reports of anti-Semitic acts or public statements by community or national leaders vilifying Jews.

Trafficking in Persons

See the Department of State's *Trafficking in Persons Report* at www.state.

Persons with Disabilities

The law provides persons with disabilities, including physical, sensory, intellectual, and mental disabilities, the same rights as other citizens in employment, education, access to health care, and the provision of other state services. However, persons with disabilities continued to face discrimination.

50   U.S. Department of State

The law mandates access to buildings for persons with disabilities, but many older buildings, including government buildings and schools, do not to conform to the law. The law also requires private enterprises employing more than 50 persons to reserve at least 2 percent of positions for persons with disabilities. In practice this regulation was not widely enforced.

There is no protective legislation to provide for equal educational opportunities for persons with disabilities.

The Ministry of Social Development is responsible for protecting the rights of persons with disabilities. The government provided alternative education opportunities for more than 500 children with disabilities, including overseas schooling when appropriate; this was largely due to lack of capacity within the country. Additionally, the Ministry of Education partnered with the International Council for Educational Reform and Development to create a curriculum for students with mental disabilities within the standard school system, which was in place throughout the year. Persons with disabilities are not restricted from voting or participating in civic affairs.

Societal Abuses, Discrimination, and Acts of Violence Based on Sexual Orientation and Gender Identity

Gay, lesbian, bisexual, and transgender (LGBT) persons faced discrimination under the law and in practice. Social norms reinforced discrimination against LGBT persons. The penal code criminalizes consensual same-sex sexual conduct with a jail term of six months to three years. There were no reports of prosecutions during the year, although nine prosecutions for sodomy occurred in 2009, the most recent year for which statistics are available.

The discussion of sexual orientation and gender identity in any context remained a social taboo, and authorities took steps to block LGBT-related Internet content. It is likely that social stigma and intimidation prevented LGBT persons from reporting incidents of violence or abuse.

Due to social conventions and potential persecution, LGBT organizations did not operate openly, nor were gay pride marches or gay rights advocacy events held. Information was not available on official or private discrimination in employment, occupation, housing, statelessness, or access to education or health care based on sexual orientation and gender identity. There were no government efforts to address potential discrimination.

Other Societal Violence or Discrimination

There were no reports of societal violence against persons with HIV/AIDS. Foreigners seeking residence in the country are tested for HIV/AIDS; they are denied a visa if they are HIV positive.

SECTION 7. WORKER RIGHTS

a. Freedom of Association and the Right to Collective Bargaining

The law protects the right of workers to form and join unions, as well as the right to conduct legal strikes and bargain collectively, with significant restrictions. The law provides for one general federation, to which all unions must affiliate, to represent unions in regional and international fora. Workers have the right to strike, but the law imposes significant restrictions. The law requires an absolute majority of an enterprise's employees to approve a strike, and notice must be given to employers three weeks in advance of the intended strike date. The law allows for collective bargaining; regulations require employers to engage in collective bargaining on the terms and conditions of employment, including wages and hours of work. Where there is no trade union, collective bargaining may take place between the employer and five representatives selected by workers. The employer may not reject any of the representatives selected. While negotiation is ongoing, the employer may not act on decisions related to issues under discussion. The law prohibits employers from firing or imposing penalties on employees for union activity, although it does not require reinstatement for workers fired for union activity. The law prohibits employers from firing or imposing penalties on employees for union activity.

Unions are open to all legal workers regardless of nationality. The law prohibits members of the armed forces, other public security institutions, government employees, and domestic workers from forming or joining unions.

The law prohibits unions from accepting grants or financial assistance from any source without the ministry's prior approval. By law unions must notify the government at least one month in advance of union meetings.

The government generally effectively enforced applicable laws. The government did not enforce the requirements for advance notice of strikes and union meetings. The government provided an alternative dispute resolution mechanism through the Ministry of Manpower, which acted as mediator between the employer and employee for minor disputes such as disagreement over wages. If not resolved to the employee's satisfaction, the employee could, and often did, resort to the courts for relief. The country lacked dedicated labor courts, and observers noted the mandatory grievance procedures were confusing to many workers, especially foreign workers.

Freedom of association in union matters and the right to collective bargaining were respected in practice. Labor unions exercised increasing independence from government, although the government paid the salaries and office expenses of federation leadership.

Strikes occurred frequently and were generally resolved quickly, sometimes through government mediation.

For example, the Ministry of Manpower and the Majlis al-Shura intervened to mediate in May when oil workers at Petroleum Development Oman and Oxy Oman went on strike.

b. Prohibition of Forced or Compulsory Labor

The law prohibits all forced or compulsory labor, and the government took steps to prevent or eliminate forced labor during the year. All police underwent training in how to identify victims of trafficking in persons to help them identify cases of forced or compulsory labor.

Conditions indicative of forced labor occurred in practice. Under the law all foreign workers must be sponsored by a citizen employer or accredited diplomatic mission. Some men and women from South and Southeast Asia, employed in the country as domestic workers or low-skilled workers in the construction, agriculture, and service sectors, faced working conditions indicative of forced labor, including withholding of passports, restrictions on movement, nonpayment of wages, long working hours without food or rest, threats, and physical or sexual abuse. Sponsorship requirements left workers vulnerable to exploitative conditions, as it was difficult for an employee to change sponsors. For example, some employers of domestic workers, contrary to law, withheld passports and other documents, complicating workers' release from unfavorable contracts and preventing workers' departure after their work contracts. In some cases, employers demanded exorbitant release fees totaling as much as 600 rials (approximately $1,560) before allowing workers to change employers. Also see the Department of State's *Trafficking in Persons Report* at www.state.

c. Prohibition of Child Labor and Minimum Age for Employment

The minimum age for employment is 15, or 18 for certain hazardous occupations. Children between the ages of 15 and 18 may only work between the hours of 6 a.m. and 6 p.m. and are prohibited from working for more than six hours per day, on weekends, or on holidays. No specific penalties are proscribed in the law for the unlawful employment of juveniles.

The Ministry of Manpower and ROP were responsible for enforcing laws with respect to child labor, and generally effectively enforced such laws in the private sector; however, enforcement often did not extend to informal and small family businesses that employed underage children, particularly in the agricultural and fishing sectors. In general minor violations resulted in warnings, and employers were given time to correct practices; however, significant violations could result in immediate arrests.

Child labor rarely occurred in practice, it was mostly in the informal economy and agricultural and fishing sectors. There were no reports of child labor during the year.

Also see the Department of Labor's *Findings on the Worst Forms of Child Labor* at www.dol.gov/ilab/programs/ocft/tda.htm.

d. Acceptable Conditions of Work

The minimum wage for citizens was 200 rials (approximately $520) per month. Minimum wage regulations did not apply to a variety of occupations and businesses, including small businesses employing fewer than five persons, dependent family members working for a family firm, or some categories of manual laborers. The minimum wage did not apply to noncitizens.

The private sector workweek was 45 hours and included a two-day rest period following five consecutive days of work. Government workers had a 35-hour workweek. The law mandates overtime pay for hours in excess of 45 per week.

The government set occupational health and safety standards. The law states an employee may leave dangerous work conditions without jeopardy to continued employment if the employer was aware of the danger and did not implement corrective measures. Employees covered under the labor law may receive compensation for job-related injury or illness through employer-provided medical insurance.

Neither wage and hour nor occupational safety and health regulations applied to domestic workers.

The Ministry of Labor was responsible for enforcing labor laws, and employed approximately 160 inspectors. It generally enforced the law effectively with respect to citizens; however, it did not effectively enforce regulations regarding hours of employment and working conditions for foreign workers.

Labor inspectors performed random checks of worksites to ensure compliance with all labor laws and had arrest authority for the most egregious violations. Approximately 180 inspectors from the Department of Health and Safety of the Labor Care Directorate generally enforced the health and safety codes and made regular on-site inspections to private sector worksites as required by law.

The ministry effectively enforced the minimum wage for citizens. In wage cases the Ministry of Manpower processed complaints and acted as mediator. In a majority of cases, the plaintiff prevailed, gaining compensation, the opportunity to seek alternative employment, or return to their country of origin in the case of foreign laborers, although they rarely used the courts to seek redress. The ministry was generally effective in cases regarding minor labor disputes; however, it did not refer any egregious violations to the courts during the year.

The government made little effort during the year to prevent violations or improve wages and working conditions, which disproportionately affected foreign workers.

Foreign workers were vulnerable to poor, dangerous, or exploitative working conditions. There were reports that migrant laborers in some firms and households worked more than 12 hours a day for below-market wages. Employers often cancelled the employment contracts of seriously sick or injured foreign workers, forcing them to return to their countries of origin or remain in the country illegally.

There are no maximum workhour limits for domestic workers, nor any mandatory rest periods, although the contract between the employer and worker can specify such requirements. Separate domestic employment regulations obligate the employer to provide domestic workers with free local medical treatment throughout the contract period. However, penalties for noncompliance with health regulations are small, ranging from approximately 10 to 100 rials (approximately $26 to $260), multiplying per occurrence per worker and doubled upon recurrence. Some domestic workers were subject to abusive conditions. For example, on November 6, the *Times of Oman* reported on a Sri Lankan house cleaner who allegedly suffered hearing loss as a result of physical abuse by her employer.

There was little data available on workplace fatalities or safety.

In: Oman: Conditions, Issues and U.S. Relations   ISBN: 978-1-62948-086-2
Editor: Sebastian Haas   © 2013 Nova Science Publishers, Inc.

Chapter 3

OMAN 2012 INTERNATIONAL RELIGIOUS FREEDOM REPORT[*]

U.S. Department of State; Bureau of Democracy, Human Rights and Labor

EXECUTIVE SUMMARY

The Basic Law prohibits discrimination based on religion and protects the right to practice religious rites on condition that doing so does not disrupt public order and, in practice, the government generally enforced these protections. The trend in the government's respect for religious freedom did not change significantly during the year. The Basic Law declares that Islam is the state religion and that Sharia (Islamic law) is the basis of legislation, although legislation is largely based on civil code. The government inconsistently enforced existing legal restrictions on the right to collective worship.

There were no reports of societal abuses or discrimination based on religious affiliation, belief, or practice.

U.S. embassy officials regularly met with officials at the Ministry of Endowment and Religious Affairs (MERA) to discuss the expansion of worship space for non-Muslim religious communities. The ambassador established relationships with leaders of religious groups in the country and encouraged the interfaith policies of the government.

---

[*] This document was released by the U.S. Department of State; Bureau of Democracy, Human Rights and Labor, May 2013.

Embassy staff spoke regularly with minority religious groups, and attended government and community interfaith and religious community events.

SECTION I. RELIGIOUS DEMOGRAPHY

A U.S. government source estimates the population at 3.1 million, 67 percent of whom are citizens. An estimated 75 percent of citizens, including Sultan Qaboos, are Ibadhi Muslims. Ibadhism is a form of Islam distinct from Shiism and the "orthodox" schools of Sunnism, and is the historically dominant religious group. Shia Muslims comprise less than 5 percent of citizens, and live mainly in the capital area and along the northern coast. The remainder of the citizen population is Sunni Muslim.

The majority of non-Muslims are foreign workers from South Asia, although there are small communities of naturalized ethnic Indians who are mainly Hindu or Christian. Non-Ibadhi religious groups constitute approximately 18 percent of the population and include Sunni and Shia Muslims and groups of Hindus, Buddhists, Sikhs, Bahais, and Christians. Christian groups are centered in the major urban areas of Muscat, Sohar, and Salalah and include Roman Catholic, Eastern Orthodox, and Protestant congregations. These groups tend to organize along linguistic and ethnic lines. There are more than 60 different Christian groups, fellowships, and assemblies active in the Muscat metropolitan area. There are also three officially recognized Hindu temples and two Sikh temples in Muscat, as well as additional temples located in foreign laborer camps.

SECTION II. STATUS OF GOVERNMENT RESPECT FOR RELIGIOUS FREEDOM LEGAL/POLICY FRAMEWORK

The Basic Law prohibits discrimination based on religion and protects the right to practice religious rites on condition that doing so does not disrupt public order. The Basic Law declares that Islam is the state religion and that Sharia is the basis of legislation, although legislation is largely based on civil code and civil courts replaced Sharia courts in 1999.

It is a criminal offense to defame any faith. The law provides for a maximum 10 years imprisonment for inciting religious or sectarian strife. The law also prescribes a maximum three-year sentence and fine of 500 rials

Oman 2012 International Religious Freedom Report

($1,300) for anyone who "publicly blasphemes God or His prophets," commits an affront to religious groups by spoken or written word, or breaches the peace of a lawful religious gathering. Using the Internet in a way that "might prejudice public order or religious values" is also a crime, with a penalty of between one month and a year in prison, and fines of not less than 1,000 rials ($2,600).

The law prohibits public proselytizing by all religious groups, although the government allows religious groups to proselytize privately within legally registered houses of worship and Islamic propagation centers.

The country's civil courts adjudicate cases governed by the Personal Status and Family Legal Code. However, the code exempts non-Muslims from its provisions in matters pertaining to family or personal status, allowing them to seek adjudication under the religious laws of their faith. Shia Muslims may resolve family and personal status cases according to Shia jurisprudence outside the courts, and retain the right to transfer their case to a civil court if they cannot find a resolution within Shia religious tradition.

Apostasy is not a criminal or civil offense per se, but the Personal Status and Family Legal Code prohibits a father who converts from Islam from retaining paternal rights over his children.

All religious organizations must register with the government. According to the MERA, there is no limit on the number of religious groups that can be registered. New religious groups unaffiliated with a previously-recognized group must gain ministerial approval before being registered. While there are no published rules, regulations, or criteria for approval, the ministry generally considers the group's size, theology, belief system, and availability of other worship opportunities before granting approval. The ministry employs similar criteria before granting approval for new Muslim groups to form.

The ministry recognizes the Protestant Church of Oman, the Catholic Diocese of Oman, the al Amana Center (inter-denominational Christian), the Hindu Mahajan Temple, and the Anwar al-Ghubaira Trading Company in Muscat (Sikh) as the official sponsors for non-Muslim religious groups. Groups seeking registration must request meeting and worship space from one of these sponsor organizations, which are responsible for recording the group's doctrinal adherence, the names of its leaders, and the number of active members, and for submitting this information to the ministry.

Leaders of all religious groups must register with MERA. The formal licensing process for imams prohibits unlicensed lay members from preaching sermons in mosques, and licensed imams must follow government-approved sermons. Lay members of non-Muslim groups may

60 U.S. Department of State

lead prayers if they are specified as leaders in their group's registration application. The ministry prohibits foreigners on tourist visas from preaching, teaching, or leading worship. The government permits clergy from abroad to enter the country to teach or lead worship under the sponsorship of registered religious groups, which must apply to MERA for approval before the visiting clergy's entry.

MERA requires religious groups to obtain approval before disseminating religious publications outside their membership; the government must approve any publication in the country. Religious groups must notify MERA before importing religious materials and submit a copy for the MERA files; however, the ministry does not review all imported religious material for approval.

Non-Muslim groups may practice their religion according to their values, customs, and traditions without interference only on land specifically donated by the sultan for the purpose of collective worship. The government does not permit gatherings for religious purposes in private homes or in any location other than government-approved houses of worship.

The government must approve construction and/or leasing of buildings by religious groups. In addition, mosques must be built at least one kilometer (0.6 mile) apart.

Although the government records religion on birth certificates, it is not printed on other official identity documents.

Women are permitted to wear the hijab (Islamic head scarf) in official photographs but not the niqab (Islamic veil that covers the face).

Citizens have the right to sue the government for violations of the right to practice religious rites that do not disrupt public order; however, this right has never been exercised in court.

Islamic studies are mandatory for Muslim students in public school grades K-12. Non-Muslim students are exempt from this requirement, and many private schools provide alternative religious studies.

The government observes the following religious holidays as national holidays: Hijra (Islamic New Year), Mawlid an-Nabi (the Birth of the Prophet Muhammad), the Prophet's Ascension, Eid al-Fitr, and Eid al-Adha.

Government Practices

There were no reports of abuses of religious freedom. The government inconsistently enforced legal restrictions on the right to collective worship.

Oman 2012 International Religious Freedom Report   61

In general, non-Muslim groups voluntarily abided by government restrictions on religious gatherings in private homes or any location other than government-approved houses of worship. Churches provided space on their compounds for worship; however, the lack of space in government-approved locations continued to limit the number of groups able to practice their religion.

The Church of Jesus Christ of Latter-day Saints (Mormons) began the registration process in 2009. At year's end, the government had not yet granted official recognition.

MERA monitored sermons at mosques to ensure imams did not discuss political topics. The government required all Ibadhi and Sunni imams to preach sermons within the parameters of standardized texts it distributed monthly.

The government funded the salaries of some Ibadhi and Sunni imams, but not of Shia or non-Muslim religious leaders.

The government promoted tolerance and interfaith understanding through continued support of an endowed professorship of Abrahamic Faiths and sponsorship of ten Omani students in a religious pluralism program at Cambridge University. The government, through MERA, continued to publish *Al Tafaham* (Understanding), a periodical devoted to broadening dialogue within Islam and promoting respectful discussion of differences with other faiths and cultures. It included articles by Christian, Muslim, Jewish, and Hindu religious scholars. The government sponsored the opening of the Center for International Dialogue in Lebanon, whose purpose was dialogue between different faiths. The government also brought many scholars of different faiths, including Christianity and Judaism, to speak on tolerance and interfaith understanding at the Grand Mosque. These lectures were given in English and Arabic.

SECTION III. STATUS OF SOCIETAL RESPECT FOR RELIGIOUS FREEDOM

There were no reports of societal abuses or discrimination based on religious affiliation, belief, or practice.

The Al Amana Center, a local interfaith group focusing on improving Muslim-Christian understanding, regularly sponsored exchange programs for leaders of Christian and Muslim communities, hosted scholars-in-residence, and worked closely with MERA on many of its projects.

SECTION IV. U.S. GOVERNMENT POLICY

U.S. embassy officials regularly met with officials at the Ministry of Endowment and Religious Affairs to discuss the expansion of worship space for non-Muslim religious groups. The ambassador established relationships with leaders of religious groups and encouraged the interfaith policies of the government. Embassy staff spoke regularly with minority religious groups, and attended government and community interfaith and religious group events. Embassy staff developed relationships with the major Christian groups in Muscat, as well as the Al Amana Center. The embassy hosted an iftar during Ramadan. Embassy staff gave tours of religious minority neighborhoods to visiting delegations. The embassy also sponsored a participant on an interfaith dialogue international visitor program.

In: Oman: Conditions, Issues and U.S. Relations   ISBN: 978-1-62948-086-2
Editor: Sebastian Haas   © 2013 Nova Science Publishers, Inc.

Chapter 4

2013 INVESTMENT CLIMATE STATEMENT: OMAN[*]

Bureau of Economic and Business Affairs

OPENNESS TO, AND RESTRICTIONS UPON, FOREIGN INVESTMENT

Oman actively seeks foreign investment and is in the process of improving the framework to encourage such investments. Oman promotes higher education, manufacturing, healthcare, aquaculture, renewable energy, ICT, and tourism as areas for investment. Investors transferring technology, developing management expertise, and providing training for Omanis are particularly welcome. The Public Authority for Investment Promotion and Export Development (PAIPED, formerly OCIPED) is tasked with attracting foreign investors and smoothing the path for business formation and private sector development. PAIPED also provides prospective foreign investors with information on government regulations, which are not always transparent and sometimes inconsistent. Although the Ministry of Commerce and Industry (MOCI) has established a 'One-Stop Shop' for government clearances, the approval process for establishing a business can be slow, particularly with respect to labor requirements for expatriate labor. In 2011, Oman experienced

---

[*] This is an edited, reformatted and augmented version of Bureau of Economic and Business Affairs publication, dated February 2013.

nationwide protests associated with the "Arab Spring," which many observers attributed to youth demands for greater economic opportunity and transparency. With more than 50 percent of the 2.9m population under 20, there is a national imperative to address the disparity between limited employment opportunities and the demographic "youth bulge". The Government of Oman (GoO) responded swiftly, decreeing the creation of 50,000 new jobs annually, the majority in the public defense and security sector, and raising the private sector minimum wage to RO 200 (US $520) per month. The minimum wage does not apply to third country nationals, and there were reports of companies switching to contract employment of foreigners to avoid mandates associated with Omani citizens. According to the Public Authority for Social Insurance, at the end of October 2012 percent83 percent of the private sector workforce earned less than RO 400 (US $ 1040) per month, and 40 percent earned below the minimum wage. By the end of 2011, there was approximately a2 percent drop in the private sector workforce as Omani citizens opted for the newly created positions in the public sector, which are perceived as being more secure and comfortable and offer higher average wages. (In 2010, for example, the average private sector worker grossed US $4,692 while the public sector counterpart earned US $19,812.)

Advantages of investing in Oman include:

- Oman's business-friendly environment, including the U.S.-Oman Free Trade Agreement; a modern business law framework; respect for free markets, contract sanctity, and property rights; relatively low taxes; and a one-stop-shop at the Ministry of Commerce and Industry for business registration;
- The educated, and largely bilingual Omani work force;
- The excellent quality of life: Oman is a safe, modern, friendly, and scenic country, with outstanding international schools, widely-available consumer goods, modern infrastructure, and a convenient and growing transportation network;
- Oman's geographic location, just outside the Persian Gulf and the Strait of Hormuz, along busy shipping lanes carrying a significant share of the world's maritime commercial traffic, with convenient access and connections to the Gulf, Africa, and the subcontinent; and,
- The steady and ambitious investment by the Government of Oman in the country's infrastructure, including free zones, seaports, airports, rail, and roads, as well as in its health care and educational systems and facilities.

In response to protester demands, the GoO also managed to finance significant increases in social subsidies (scholarships, wage supports, housing allowances,) thanks to prevailing high oil prices, averaging US $102 per barrel in 2011, and still enjoy a budget surplus of US $2.2bn at the end of 2011. In 2012, the GoO announced a US $26bn budget (a 9percent increase in spending) with robust increases in education, health, public employment, and social spending. The 2013 budget follows this trend, with a 16 percent increase in social security and welfare payments, paired with a 16 percent increase for education, 32 percent increase for health, and 45 percent increase for housing. The budgeted oil reference price in 2011 was US $75 (up from the previous US $58 reference price), increased again to US $85 for the 2013 budget, but if current global trends continue to keep oil close to US $100 per barrel the GoO should have no problem paying for the new benefits and maintaining a budget surplus.

With the implementation of the U.S.-Oman Free Trade Agreement (FTA) on January 1, 2009, U.S. firms may establish and fully own a business in Oman without a local partner. U.S.-Oman FTA commitments have increased opportunities for U.S. financial service providers, as well as cross-border service providers in the areas of communications, express delivery, computer-related technologies, health care, and distribution, among others. Other (i.e., non-U.S.) majority foreign-owned entrants are barred from most professional service areas, including engineering, architecture, law, and accountancy. There are some exceptions for international consultancies, though requirements are strict. For example, engineering consultancies must be 35 percent owned by an Omani who is currently practicing in the specialized field with a relevant degree and the foreign partner is required to possess a minimum of ten years' experience in the field before MOCI will approve a license. Although U.S. investors are provided national treatment in most sectors, Oman has an exception in the FTA for legal services, limiting U.S.-ownership in a legal services firm to no more than 70 percent. In addition, Oman has limited foreign lawyers to practicing in appeals courts, with the goal of phasing them out entirely in the court system; many expatriates continue to work as corporate lawyers and advisors however, and arbitration is widely used. In 2011, Oman also began to enforce a new directive limiting customs clearing and forwarding activities to Omani and GCC citizens. Oman has not historically had a provision in its commercial legal framework for the establishment of a foreign-owned branch except for the purpose of responding to a government tender; discussions on how to register American branches outside of the widely used LLC format are ongoing.

The Foreign Capital Investment Law (Royal Decree No. 102/94) provides the legal framework for non-U.S. and non-GCC foreign investors. Oman amended this law in 2000 as part of its WTO accession and in 2009 to implement the U.S.-Oman Free Trade Agreement. For most investments (apart from those covered by the FTA) the law requires that there be at least 35percent Omani ownership. There are exceptions; notably wholly foreign-owned branches of foreign banks are allowed to enter the market. Non-American investors may also obtain approval by the Ministerial Cabinet to allow a 100 percent foreign-owned business entity if the investment is in the national interest. Aside from ensuring that the investor satisfies the legal requirements for entry into the market, Oman does not screen foreign investment. If a concern were raised regarding a particular investor's entry into the market, the MOCI would be the government body tasked with reviewing the proposed investor. Investments are not screened for competition considerations, and Oman does not have an active competition commission.

Oman has privatized some parastatal corporations and is in the process of privatizing others, but maintains government dominance in several sectors. In 2011 the government amended legislation to allow for public-private partnerships in government hospitals and clinics, paving the way for significant private investment in planned "medical cities" in Salalah and Muscat. Foreign investors are allowed to participate fully in privatization programs, even in drafting public-private partnership frameworks. The most successful privatization program to-date has been the electricity and desalination privatization program. The telecommunications sector has also been increasingly privatized. Industrial establishments must be licensed by MOCI. In addition, a foreign firm interested in establishing a company in Oman must obtain relevant approvals from other ministries, such as the Ministry of Environment and Climate Affairs and organizations such as the Oman Chamber of Commerce and Industry. Foreign workers must obtain work permits and residency permits from the Ministry of Manpower and the Royal Oman Police-Immigration. To speed the approval process, MOCI created a "One-Stop-Shop" where representatives from relevant ministries are present to receive inquiries, forms, and applications. However the authentication of foreign registration documents (Certificate of Incorporation, Articles of Association, Board resolution to participate in the new company, and Power of Attorney appointing one or more individuals to sign the constitutive contract) is a time-consuming process which has frustrated many investors. Oman has a flat tax of 12 percent for all businesses; the first US $78,000 in profits is tax exempt. (This differs for oil and gas investors, whose taxes are negotiated in individual mining concession agreements.) Duty and tax exemptions are granted for renewable five year periods for investments in manufacturing, mining, agriculture, aquaculture, tourism, locally manufactured exports, education and healthcare. There are no taxes on personal income, capital gains, or inheritance. There are a few minor municipality taxes on lease agreements, hotel and leisure facilities etc. Foreign airlines and shipping companies are completely exempt from taxation based upon reciprocal treatment by foreign governments. Higher education institutes, private sector schools, training institutes, and private hospitals are also tax exempt. The free zones in Duqm, Salalah and Sohar offer renewable five year tax holidays. In 2012, the Secretariat General for Taxation at the Ministry of Finance established a Large Taxpayer Unit to increase focus on large taxpayers while improving their service. Commercial law in Oman is continually evolving. Although the judicial process is slow, business contracts are generally enforced. According to the 2013 World Bank Ease of Doing Business Report, it takes an average of 598 days to enforce a business contract. However, the cost of enforcement is a smaller percentage of the claim, at 13.5 percent, lower than even OECD countries, which average 20 percent. Insolvency laws are nascent, at this time allowing only for complete dissolution rather than restructuring, and many businesses opt to simply shut their doors rather than go through the insolvency process, which can take up to four years. The U.S. Department of Commerce has provided comments to draft updates of Oman's Commercial Companies Law and Capital Markets Law encouraging modernized bankruptcy legislation to allow for appropriate reorganization. Omani law currently provides for arrest and imprisonment in many bankruptcy cases. Oman recently adopted an e-Commerce law although it has yet to be tested in the court system. In 2012 the Public Authority for Consumer Protection and the Public Authority for Stores and Food Reserves implemented price controls on staple foods and consumer products to counter inflation, causing many companies to suffer losses.

The current process for registering a business in Oman is laid out in the Foreign Investment Law (promulgated by Royal Decree No. 102/94) as per below. In late 2011 PAIPED requested U.S. government assistance to begin revising and updating the law. The current requirements include:

1) Submit an application duly signed by at least three founders in case of Joint Stock Companies, and by at least two members in case of other types of Companies.

2) Submit a certificate from the Commercial Registration stating that no other Company is registered in Oman under the same proposed commercial name.
3) Prepare the Articles of Association/Incorporation of the proposed Company, according to its legal type.
4) If a proposed partner is a juristic person (corporate entity with legal standing), it must submit its Articles of Association and Certificate of Registration and Power of Attorney to its authorized Managers. In case of a non-Omani juristic person, also a brochure of the Company's major projects and last balance sheet (if any) are preferred to be submitted as well, duly attested (as well as the former) by the concerned authorities in the country where the head office of the Company is located and from the Embassy of Oman there.
5) Capital of the proposed Company should not be less than RO 150,000 (US $390,000). *(Note: US Companies subject to local requirement of RO 20,000 as per FTA national treatment provision.)*
6) Omani proportion in the Capital and share of profit should not be less than 35percent. *(Note: US Companies exempted under FTA.)*
7) Activities and objects of the proposed Company should be limited within one specific field. No foreign participation is allowed in General Trade and Service ventures.
8) The non-Omani partner other than citizens of Gulf Cooperation Council (GCC) States in the proposed Company must be a Juristic Person having an experience of not less than 5 years in the same field of the activity required.
9) Written approvals must be obtained from the appropriate government departments concerned with the proposed activities.
10) When the establishment of the Company is approved, the necessary financial recommendations are to be forwarded and steps for registering with the Commercial Registry are to be taken.

OMAN'S INTERNATIONAL RANKINGS

Measure

2011 Transparency International Perceptions of Corruption Index: 4.8/10*
2011 Heritage Foundation Index of Economic Freedom: 69.8/100**
2012 World Bank Ease of Doing Business Indicator: 49th/183 countries

*0: "Highly Corrupt" to 10: "Very Clean"
**100: "Maximum Economic Freedom"

In its 'Doing Business 2013' report, released on October 23, the World Bank assessed a total of 185 economies, with Oman maintaining its rank at 47th, placing well above the Middle East and North Africa (MENA) average of 98, and fifth among all Arab states. The annual survey sets out 10 separate criteria for the world's economies: starting a business, dealing with construction permits, getting electricity, registering property, obtaining credit, protecting investors, paying taxes, trading across borders, enforcing contracts and resolving insolvency. Oman posted improvements in four categories, no change in one and slight falls in the remaining five.

In terms of starting a business, Oman regressed six places, though this has more to do with the fact that other countries have implemented reforms, making it easier to launch an enterprise, rather than the Sultanate making it more difficult. Indeed, over the past six years, Oman has reduced the number of steps necessary to start a business from 10 to 5, while the number of days required to complete the necessary procedures has fallen from 35 to 8.

One area where Oman recorded a solid advance was in the ease of obtaining credit, climbing 14 rungs on the ladder to 83rd. This is a reflection of strong capitalization of local banks and low interest rates set by the Central Bank of Oman. The reserve's policy of keeping rates around 1percent has encouraged commercial banks to ease their own lending criteria, which in turn has had a positive flow into the private sector.

Oman also maintained its position as the 32nd most competitive country in the 2012/13 World Economic Forum's Global Competitiveness Index, a measure of the economies of 144 countries. This ranking places Oman in the top 25 percentile of the world's economies and ranks it above economic powerhouses including India, South Africa, Italy and Turkey.

Conversion and Transfer Policies

Oman does not have restrictions or reporting requirements on private capital movements into or out of the country. There are no plans to change remittance policies. Oman does not restrict the remittance abroad of equity or debt capital, interest, dividends, branch profits, royalties, management and service fees, and personal savings. The Omani Rial is pegged at a rate of RO 0.3849 to the U.S. dollar, and there is no difficulty in obtaining exchange. The government has consistently, firmly, and publicly stated that it is committed to maintaining the current peg. The GoO has stated firmly it will not join the proposed GCC common currency. There is no delay in remitting investment returns or limitation on the inflow or outflow of funds for remittances of profits, debt service, capital, capital gains returns on intellectual property, or imported inputs. Investors can remit through legal parallel markets utilizing convertible, negotiable instruments. There are no surrender requirements for profits earned overseas.

The Central Bank of Oman (CBO) regulates local banks on all lending practices to individuals and corporations inside the Sultanate. In May 2011, Oman approved the introduction of Islamic banking to the Sultanate. Regulations governing the new sector will be issued by CBO in early 2012. Omani financial institutions, controlled by a strong and effective regulatory system, are well-capitalized, have low non-performing loan ratios, and tend to report attractive profits. Individuals have to be resident in Oman or have an investor visa to open a bank account and transfer funds. For foreign bank transfers, Omani banks require complete documentation of the source of funds before approving the transaction.

Expropriation and Compensation

Oman's interest in increased foreign investment and technology transfer make expropriation or nationalization unlikely, although there have been sporadic reports of these in the past several years. In the event that a property must be nationalized, e.g., for a public building, Article 11 of the Basic Law of the State stipulates that the Government of Oman must provide prompt and fair compensation. There are no recent examples of expropriations, although on December 8, 2011 the first trade dispute under the U.S.-Oman FTA was submitted to formal arbitration at the World Bank's International Center for Settlement of Investment Disputes. The complainant filed an initial intent to arbitrate on April 4, 2011, claiming expropriation of his multi-million dollar investment in a mining operation by the Oman Mining Company after he was arrested for allegedly mining without necessary permits. The matter is ongoing. (Under the U.S.-Oman Free Trade Agreement, Oman must follow international standards for expropriation and compensation cases, including access to international arbitration.) In practice, Oman compensates for any expropriations it makes, although at times the compensation can be incrementally paid. There are no laws forcing local ownership in any sector,

2013 Investment Climate Statement: Oman

though land ownership is limited to Omani and GCC nationals outside of special Integrated Tourism Complexes set aside for foreign residency. (The U.S.-Oman FTA excludes land ownership.)

Dispute Settlement

Oman is a party to the International Convention for the Settlement of Investment Disputes between States and Nationals of other States (ICSID) and the UN New York Convention of 1958 on the Recognition and Enforcement of Foreign Arbitral Awards. Oman's legal framework provides for the enforcement of international arbitration awards and most foreign companies elect for dispute resolution by arbitration. Arbitration is generally cheaper, quicker and easier than settling commercial disputes in the normal court system, where judges often lack expertise on technical commercial issues. Business disputes within Oman are resolved through the Commercial Court. The Commercial Court has jurisdiction over most tax and labor cases, and can issue orders of enforcement of decisions. The Commercial Court can also accept cases against governmental bodies; however, the Court can only issue, and not enforce, rulings against the government. If the value of the case is less than US $26,000, the Commercial Court's decision is final. If the value exceeds US $26,000, the case is taken up by a Court of Appeal. Parties may appeal their case to the Supreme Court. Cases can only be reopened after judgment if new documents are discovered or irregularities (e.g., forgery, perjury) are found. There is no provision for the publication of decisions, apart from arbitrations carried out under the U.S.-Oman FTA, and the decisions do not carry precedent. U.S. firms should note that the Commercial Court is relatively new, replacing the Authority for Settlement of Commercial Disputes, and many practical details regarding the new Court have yet to be finalized.

Oman has written and consistently applied commercial and bankruptcy laws, though the U.S. Department of Commerce is providing expertise to help the GoO update them. According to the World Bank, it takes on average four years to resolve bankruptcy and investors can expect to recover 36.6 cents on their dollar. However, the expense of resolving bankruptcy is significantly lower in Oman than the region. Would-be investors should note that Omani law (Royal Decree 55/1990) provides for civil arrest and imprisonment in many bankruptcy cases.

Oman maintains other judicial bodies to adjudicate various disputes. The Labor Welfare Board under the Ministry of Manpower hears disputes regarding severance pay, wages, benefits, etc. The Real Estate Committee hears tenant-landlord disputes, the Police Committee deals with traffic matters, and the Magistrate Court handles misdemeanors and criminal matters. All litigation and hearings are conducted in Arabic. Binding international arbitration of investment disputes between foreign investors and the Omani government is recognized. Omani courts recognize and enforce foreign arbitral awards, and international arbitration is accepted as a means to settle investment disputes between private parties.

The Oman Chamber of Commerce and Industry has an arbitration committee to which parties to a dispute may refer their case when the amounts in question are small. Local authorities, including 'walis' (district governors appointed by the central government), also handle minor disputes. Although Oman is a member of the GCC Arbitration Center, located in Bahrain, the Center is not yet firmly established and is not widely used. The Bahrain Center for Dispute Resolution, a member of the American Arbitration Association (AAA) in New York, is very active in the region.

In 2011, a U.S. investor brought the first investment dispute case against the GoO for arbitration under the FTA and proceedings are ongoing.

Performance Requirements and Incentives

Oman is subject to trade related investment measures (TRIMs) obligations. At this time, there are no allegations that Oman maintains any measures that violate the WTO TRIM text.

Oman offers several incentives to attract foreign investors. These include:

- A five-year tax holiday, renewable once for an additional five years;
- Subsidized plant facilities and utilities at industrial estates;
- Exemption from customs duties on equipment and raw materials during the first ten years of a project, with packaging materials exempted for five years;
- English as an accepted *lingua franca* for business contracts and operations;
- A low corporate tax rate, capped at 12 percent; and
- No personal income or capital gains tax.

Firms involved in agriculture and fishing, industry, education and training, healthcare, mining, export manufacturing, tourism, and public utilities are eligible for the renewable 5-year tax holiday and exemption from duties on capital goods and raw materials.

Under the Industry Organization and Encouragement Law of 1978, incentives are available to licensed industrial installations on the recommendation of the Industrial Development Committee. "Industrial installations" include not only those for the conversion of raw materials and semi-finished parts into manufactured products, but also mechanized assembly and packaging operations.

Omani and American-owned commercial enterprises, and foreign industrial producers in joint venture with local firms that produce goods locally, need to meet standard quality specifications. The government offers subsidies to offset the cost of feasibility and other studies if the proposed project is considered sufficiently important to the national economy. Only in the most general sense of business plan objectives does proprietary information have to be provided to qualify for incentives.

Foreign investors do not need to purchase from local sources or export a certain percentage of output. Foreign investors have access to local and foreign exchange for export finance. Offsets on civilian government procurements are rare, and are generally limited to procurements by the Ministry of Defense, Royal Oman Police, or Ministry of the Royal Office.

U.S. and foreign firms are able to participate in government financed/subsidized research programs on a national treatment basis, and are at times solicited.

Foreign firms operating in Oman, including U.S. companies, must meet "Omanization" requirements, which require businesses to employ a percentage of Omani citizens as determined by the Ministry of Manpower. On November 15, 2011, the U.S. Department of Commerce initiated antidumping (AD) and countervailing duty (CVD) investigations of circular welded carbon-quality steel pipe (steel pipe) imported from Oman.

On December 9, 2011, the U.S. International Trade Commission (ITC) preliminarily determined that there is a reasonable indication that a U.S. industry is materially injured by reason of imports of steel pipe from Oman that are allegedly sold in the United States at less than fair value and subsidized by the Government of Oman.

Commerce eventually found on November 14, 2012 that injury to domestic industry was not sufficient to warrant continuing the case. In 2010,

74 Bureau of Economic and Business Affairs

imports of steel pipe from Oman were valued at an estimated US $24.2 million.

A full list of incentives is laid out in the Foreign Investment Law as follows:

1) Interest-free loans by Government under Royal Decree No. 83/80 concerning the financial support to the private sector in agriculture, fisheries, industry, mining and quarrying and Royal Decree No. 40/87 of the financial support to the private sector in Industry and Tourism.

2) Low interest loans to industrial firms from the Oman Development Bank.

3) Exemption from customs duties on imports of equipment and raw materials required for production purposes.

4) Tariff protection through imposition or increase of customs duties on imported goods similar to local products or to prohibit or restrict their importation, taking into consideration the quality and quantity of local production and the interest of the consumer. The list of products currently under protection includes some types of pipes, cement, cement-products, paints, polyurethane products, corrugated cartons, vegetable oil, detergents and chain-link fencing. *(Note: Some of this support is currently being challenged by foreign competitors under WTO rules.)*

5) Exemption from corporate tax for a period of five years which can be renewed for another period of five years starting from the date of permission of registration of production commencement.

6) Planned and serviced industrial plots for setting up factories.

7) Recommendation to the Ministry of Electricity and Water for the reduction of utility charges for industrial purposes for those industries fulfilling the conditions for reduction.

8) Survey of industrial investment opportunities and preparation of feasibility studies important to national economy.

Right to Private Ownership and Establishment

Oman's commercial companies law requires that all actions by private entities to establish, acquire, and dispose of interests in business enterprises be announced in the commercial register, and are subject to the approval of

MOCI. Foreign and domestic firms can engage in most commercial activities after obtaining a business license from the MOCI.

Protection of Property Rights

Securitized interests in property, both moveable and real, are recognized and enforced in Oman. Foreign nationals are able to obtain mortgages on land in designated Integrated Tourism Complexes. Individuals record their interest in property with the Land Registry at the Ministry of Housing. The legal system, in general, facilitates the acquisition and disposition of property rights.

Oman is a member of the World Intellectual Property Organization (WIPO) and is registered as a signatory to the Madrid, Paris and Berne conventions on trademarks and intellectual property protection. Oman has also signed the WIPO Copyright Treaty and the WIPO Performances and Phonograms Treaty. Oman is also a signatory to the International Convention for the Protection of New Varieties of Plants. Trademark laws in Oman are Trade Related aspects of Intellectual Property Rights (TRIPs) compliant. Trademarks are valid for ten years while patents are generally protected for twenty years. As "literary works", software and audiovisual content is protected for fifty years.

Transparency of Regulatory System

Because commercial registration and licensing decisions often require the approval of multiple ministries, the government decision-making process can be tedious and may be perceived as non-transparent. Obtaining licenses for some business activities, particularly labor certifications, can be time consuming and complicated for foreign companies, as the various ministries from which licensure is required do not widely disseminate their policies, quotas, and regulations. In 2011 and 2012 U.S. investors complained about delays in receiving approvals for new mining exploration licenses. The Ministry of Commerce and Industry (MOCI) extended a moratorium on new licenses; the freeze had been imposed due to speculation of mining plots. Investors complain the MOCI should separate permitting for simple quarrying activities, the majority of applications, from large scale mineral concessions involving millions of dollars of capital expenditure. They claim bureaucracy in the licensing and environmental permitting process is deterring investment at a time of high commodity prices.

Oman's labor laws, which require minimum quotas of Omani employees depending on the type of work, form another potential impediment to foreign investment. The government's Omanization effort has been the subject of criticism in the Omani private sector, which sees it as harmful to productivity and restrictive of firms' hiring and firing policies. U.S. companies are not exempt from Omanization requirements under the FTA. Omanization requirements increased after protests in February, March, and April of 2011, and included an obligation to provide a minimum wage and more training programs for Omani employees.

The government occasionally publishes proposed laws and regulations for public comment, particularly laws that may affect the private sector. However, the Oman Chamber of Commerce and Industry complained that new mandates in the revised labor law were imposed with no consultation or grace period in late 2011. There has been a move in recent years towards greater transparency in telecommunications, securities, and corporate governance of publicly traded companies. The Telecom industry is regulated by the Telecommunications Regulatory Authority (TRA). The TRA oversees the process of liberalization and privatization of the telecommunications sector. In order to meet Oman's FTA commitments, the TRA has issued new procedures for businesses to qualify for Class I licenses and has submitted for public comment its proposal to issue Class II licenses.

Oman has also improved the transparency of its securities markets and publicly traded companies largely through the work of the Capital Markets Authority (CMA), the regulatory body for such areas. The CMA requires all public companies to comply with a set of standards for disclosure. Under the requirements, holding companies must publish the accounts of their subsidiaries with the parent companies' accounts. Companies must fully disclose their investment portfolios, including details of the purchase cost and current market prices for investment holdings. The new initiatives also require publication of these financial statements in the local press. At the same time, the Central Bank has introduced new rules to limit the level of "related party transactions" (financial transactions involving families or subsidiary companies belonging to major shareholders or board members) in Oman's commercial banks. The new rules will help increase transparency in financial transactions in local banks and the Muscat Securities Market (MSM), and will help clarify the activities of publicly-traded companies. The CMA has also moved to shorten the time period companies have to file their financial

2013 Investment Climate Statement: Oman

statements after the close of the fiscal year from three months to two, shorten the time period in which companies have to hold their annual meeting after the close of the fiscal year from four months to three, and require that an internal audit be completed for joint stock companies with capital of over five million RO (US $ 13 million).

Efficient Capital Markets and Portfolio Investment

There are no restrictions in Oman on the flow of capital and the repatriation of profits. Foreigners may invest in the Muscat Securities Market (MSM) so long as they do so through an authorized broker. Access to Oman's limited commercial credit resources is open to Omani firms with some foreign participation. At this time, there is not sufficient liquidity in the market to allow for the entry and exit of sizeable amounts of capital. Joint stock companies with capital in excess of US $5.2 million must be listed on the MSM.

According to the recently amended Commercial Companies Law, companies must have been in existence for at least two years before being floated for public trading. Private, publicly traded firms in Oman are still a relatively new phenomenon. (The Muscat Securities Market was founded in 1988.) Publicly traded firms remain a minority of businesses, the majority remaining family enterprises. The banking system is sound and well-capitalized with low levels of non-performing loans and generally high profits. Banks' portfolios are dominated by personal loans, perceived as safe as they are typically drawn directly from borrowers' government salaries. The government finances most infrastructure projects. As a surplus nation enjoying high prices on oil exports, the GoO issues few bonds and private investment and pension funds typically invest in real estate, manufacturing, and limited projects outside the country.

Typical security provided is as follows:

- mortgage over land (owned, usufruct or lease)
- commercial mortgage (over assets of company)
- share pledge (for joint stock companies only)
- parent company guarantees
- bank guarantees / letters of credit

Competition from State-Owned Enterprises

Oman has been a regional leader in the privatization of utilities, especially power, water and waste management. In general, private enterprises are allowed to compete with public enterprises under the same terms and conditions with access to markets, and other business operations, such as licenses and supplies. Public enterprises, however, have comparatively better access to credit. State-Owned Enterprises (SOEs) are active in a variety of fields, namely utilities, telecommunications, the national airline, and food production. Board membership of SOEs is composed of various government officials, with a senior official, usually cabinet-level, and serving as chairperson.

Oman has two sovereign wealth funds; the General Reserve Fund of the Sultanate of Oman, and the Oman Investment Fund. The majority of the Funds' assets are invested abroad, although their dealings are opaque. Omani sovereign wealth funds are not required by law to publish an annual report or submit their books for an independent audit.

Corporate Social Responsibility

There is a general awareness of corporate social responsibility (CSR) among businesses in Oman. Several companies routinely host competitions in elementary and secondary schools for academic performance and artistic skill; many sponsor charitable, academic and social events.

The larger Omani firms have CSR policies; however, most of Oman's smaller enterprises do not knowingly follow CSR principles such as the OECD Guidelines for Multinational Enterprises. Foreign companies operating in Oman, however, are generally OECD compliant. Firms that pursue CSR are viewed favorably.

Political Violence

Politically motivated violence is rare in Oman. Some incidents of violence were associated with demonstrations in February, March, and April 2011, although most protests were peaceful. The government allows peaceful demonstrations to occur, but any public protest event is rare.

Corruption

Ministers are not allowed to hold offices in public shareholding companies or serve as chairperson of a closely held company. However, many influential figures in government maintain private business interests and some are also involved in private-public projects. These activities either create or have the potential to create conflicts of interest. In 2011, the Tender Law was updated to preclude Tender Board officials from adjudicating projects involving interested relatives to "the second degree of kinship". In 2012, 30 cases involving financial irregularities and misuse of influence in awarding of government contracts were referred to the Public Prosecutor by the State Financial and Administrative Audit Institution.

Most major contracts are awarded through a slow and rigorous tender process governed by Oman's Tender Board. Pursuant to the U.S.-Oman FTA, Oman advertises most tenders in the local press, international periodicals, and on the Tender Board's website, although a few sensitive projects are not publicized and not subject to FTA obligations. Also, bidders are now requested to be present at the opening of bids, and interested parties may view the process on the Tender Board's website. Disputes arising from the tendering process are reviewed domestically.

Sultan Qaboos has dismissed several ministers and senior government officials for corruption during his reign. In one of Oman's biggest corruption scandals in several years, over 30 government and private sector employees, including the Under Secretary of the Ministry of Housing, Electricity, and Water, were convicted in October 2005 on counts of bribery and forgery, among others. There was also a major reshuffle after the protests in early 2011 and the State Audit Institution, renamed the "State Financial and Administrative Audit Institution" was granted expanded powers under Royal Decree 27/2011.

The institution's mandates now encompass the following:

- to secure public funds, provide a framework for efficient management of such funds, and ensure their efficient and optimal utilization;
- to detect financial and administrative irregularities and identify inherent deficiencies in the relevant financial and administrative laws;
- to identify the causes of, and assign responsibility for, any deficient performances; and

- to ensure transparency in financial and administrative transactions, and make recommendations for the avoidance of conflict of interests and for the prevention of financial and/or administrative irregularities.

In 2012, the Government announced that public sector employees would be subject to financial disclosure requirements. Oman has not yet signed the UN Convention against Corruption, though it is an observer and the government has set up a committee to consider and prepare for membership.

Bilateral Investment Agreements

Oman is a member of the Gulf Cooperation Council, which is in the process of finalizing Free Trade Agreements with the European Union, Malaysia, and Singapore. While enjoying a Free Trade Agreement, Oman does not have a bilateral taxation treaty with the U.S., however, in 2012, the Government of Oman formally requested to begin treaty negotiations. Omani tax authorities may allow relief for foreign taxes paid, limited to the Omani 12percent tax rate. Oman has signed double taxation treaties with many countries including: Algeria, Belarus, Belgium, Brunei, Canada, China, Croatia, Egypt, France, India, Iran, Italy, Mauritius, Morocco, Moldova, Netherlands, Pakistan, Russia, Seychelles, Singapore, South Africa, South Korea, Sudan, Syria, Tanzania, Thailand, Turkey, Tunisia, the United Kingdom, Uzbekistan, Vietnam and Yemen.

OPIC and Other Investment Insurance Programs

Oman is eligible for Export-Import Bank of the United States (EXIM) financing as well as Overseas Private Investment Corporation (OPIC) insurance coverage. Unusual for a Gulf country, Oman provides export credit insurance against commercial and political risk, through the Oman Development Bank, as well as the independent Export Credit Guarantee Agency of Oman, a closed stock company which has helped facilitate the dramatic rise in non-oil exports to over 100 countries over the last 20 years through extending credit insurance, guarantees and financial support to Omani exporters. The U.S. Embassy in Muscat purchases local currency at the fixed rate of 1 Omani Rial to US $ 2.60. Due to the likelihood of continuing high oil

2013 Investment Climate Statement: Oman

prices, there is very little risk of devaluation or depreciation of the Omani rial in the next year.

Labor

Oman's 2003 Labor Law governs employee/employer relations in the private sector, and enumerates the protections afforded all legally resident workers. The law sets the minimum working age at 15, provides clear guidelines on working hours, and specifies the penalties for noncompliance with its provisions. Work rules must be approved by the Ministry of Manpower and posted conspicuously in the work place. The labor law and subsequent regulations also detail requirements for occupational safety and access to medical treatment. Working conditions in Oman for many blue-collar expatriate workers are difficult, due to low wages, hot weather conditions, long hours, and social isolation. Expatriates, mainly from Western countries, fill many managerial positions. In large part to qualify for eligibility for the FTA, Oman in 2006 made significant amendments to the 2003 Labor Law. The amendments and associated Ministerial Decisions allow for more than one union per firm, require employers to engage in collective bargaining over terms and conditions of employment, and specify guidelines for conducting strikes. The amendments also prohibit employers from firing or otherwise penalizing workers for engaging in union activity, and increase the penalties for hiring underage workers or engaging in forced labor. As a result, about 100 unions were registered, covering both Omanis and expatriates.

While unions appear to be making strides in their advocacy efforts for workers, management in the major industrial free zones in Sohar and Salalah remains frustrated with ambiguity in the labor law. For example, business leaders in Salalah noted that the labor code was written for traditional retail and office jobs. The industrial jobs that dominate in Salalah require different (and technically illegal) hours and schedules, leaving these workers in a legal limbo, without clear coverage by the law. In any case, unions report that workers are satisfied and have even sent away Ministry of Manpower inspectors. Management also noted that workers ask for concessions and privileges given to the public sector (housing allowances, free loans, and generous pensions, for example). (Note: Oman's labor law provides for unions only in the private sector.) Management in Sohar and Salalah expressed additional concerns about the labor law's lack of clarity on a number of issues. The labor law was first published in 1973 and updated only intermittently, without explanation or clarifications. For example, there is no specificity in the law regarding what an employer must pay to an employee who is injured in a workplace accident that is his own fault. Management believes that they should not be held responsible for such accidents, while the law seems to hold that in any accident, no matter how negligent the employee who causes it, the employer is to blame. Another contentious example surrounds bonuses; the law suggests that bonuses must be paid every year, regardless of the company's profit margins. Management argues that companies without a profit should not be forced to pay bonuses.

On October 26, 2011, Sultan Qaboos issued Royal Decree No 113/2011 amending provisions in the Labor Law to provide increased protections and rights to the private sector workforce including shorter workweeks, fully paid maternity leave, and increases in overtime pay. The business sector has expressed concern about the increased costs of implementing many of these changes. The changes are expected to primarily affect only Omani citizen workers; expatriate workers are often hesitant to assert their rights out of concern that their employment contracts might be allowed to lapse, requiring them to leave Oman.

The most important changes to the Labor Law include:

- If the ownership of a project partially or wholly changes hands, the new owner must continue to employ the previous Omani workforce at their previous salaries;
- Direct deposit receipt is the only proof of payment of salary;
- 30 days annual paid leave (up from 15) after six months continuous work (down from one year) and six days paid emergency leave (up from four). A worker may not waive his or her leave;
- Overtime begins to accrue after 45 hours of work in one week (down from 48) or more than nine hours in one day;
- During Ramadan, Muslim workers shall not be required to work more than 30 hours a week (down from 36) or 6 hours a day;
- Overtime day work will be paid at 25 percent above the normal salary rate; night work and Friday work at 50 percent;
- Every worker must receive two paid days of rest (up from 24 hours) after five continuous days of work;
- Women may not be required to work between the hours of nine p.m. to six a.m. (previously seven p.m. to seven a.m.) *(Note: This rule is subject to multiple exceptions as published by the Ministry of*

Manpower, such as health workers, transportation workers, and women working in certain petrochemical fields.)

- Paid maternity leave of 50 days up to three times per woman per employer (up from 42 days of unpaid leave);
- Unlawfully discharged workers (as determined by the courts) will receive a minimum of three months of their gross wage and any severance pay to which they were due in the original work contract;
- New penalties for failure to adhere to Omanization rates.

The minimum wage for Omani citizens working in the private sector, including salary and benefits, was increased by Royal Decree in February 2011 from RO 120 (US $312) to RO 200 (US $520) per month. Omani employees must also receive a monthly RO10 (US $26) accommodation allowance and a RO10 transportation allowance. There is no minimum wage for non-Omanis. On January 30, 2012, the government of Oman issued Ministerial Decision 32/2012 requiring a yearly minimum increment of 3 percent for all employees with satisfactory performance who have been employed more than six months. This was in order to ensure wages keep up with inflation, but has been met with resistance to implementation among many companies. In its annual compensation and benefits report for Oman, Hay Group noted that the average salary increase in 2012 was 3.9 per cent, down from the 2011 figure of 6.2 percent. The rise in salaries has predominantly taken the form of an increment on basic salary which rose 5.7 per cent, on average, rather than adding to allowances such as housing, transport and education. According to the report, Oman's oil and gas sector had the highest pay rises of seven percent, on average, this year.

Participation in the Public Authority for Social Insurance (PASI) scheme is mandatory for all employers employing Omanis. Employees are covered for old age, disability, occupational and non-occupational injuries and death. The employer and employee are required to contribute 9.5 percent and 6.5 percent respectively of the basic salary to the fund every month and every employer must pay a further 1 percent as security against occupational injuries and diseases. For foreign employees who are not beneficiaries of PASI, End of Service Benefits (EOSB) are calculated per the Labor Law. EOSB is computed as being equal to 15 days basic wages for each year in the first three years of service, and one month for each of the following years. The EOSB is calculated on the basis of the final basic salary. No EOSB is payable if the period of service is less than one year or the employee was dismissed without notice, e.g., for serious cause in accordance with the Labor Law. The Labor

84 Bureau of Economic and Business Affairs

Law provides for, but does not require, a three month probationary period, in which either party may terminate the contract with seven days notice. For indefinite contracts, employment may be terminated by either party with 30 days notice (waived if compensation equal to the salary for the notice period is paid instead).

The government's Omanization initiative, a quota system mandating hiring of specified percentages of Omani citizens, is a high priority for the government. Approximately 50,000 young Omanis enter the workforce each year. Most of these new entries seek government employment, and Omanis make up 84 percent of the public sector's labor force. Only 18 percent of the private workforce is Omani. Organizations with more than 50 employees are expected to set aside the following "Omanized" positions for citizens: HR Manager, Security Officers, Secretarial / Administrative Clerks, Public Relations Officers, and Drivers.

Current Omanization rates for selected sectors are as follows:

- Information Technology
  - Senior Management 9 percent
  - Sales and Marketing 100 percent
  - Technical Support and Infrastructure 15 percent
  - Applications and Services Development 15 percent
- Consultancy Services
  - Engineers 25 percent
  - Draftsman 70 percent
  - Material Supervision 45 percent
  - Land Survey 80 percent
  - Accountants 60 percent
  - Administrative Posts 90 percent
- Oil & Gas 82-90 percent
- Telecom 54-80 percent
- Finance and Insurance Sector 45-90 percent

As part of a package of incentives for foreign investors, Oman's Free Zones allow for lower Omanization rates. Pressure to meet Omanization goals significantly increased as a result of protests in early 2011. The Ministry of Manpower will not issue a labor clearance for companies that fail to hire qualified Omanis to meet the labor targets. If qualified Omanis are not available, the Ministry may issue labor clearances pending future availability of qualified Omanis to fill such positions. The Ministry also assists companies in training Omanis for high-demand positions if the companies agree to hire them once trained. Under the U.S.-Oman FTA, the Omani government may set Omanization targets of up to 80 percent for U.S. companies in the Sultanate, excluding managers, board members, and specialty personnel. Private companies have expressed concerns about the work ethic of Omanis compared with expatriate staff, as well as absenteeism of local workers who are harder to dismiss because of the protections they enjoy under local employment laws. However the Ministry of Manpower is authorized to impose fines for companies that don't achieve targets. These fines can reach up to 50 percent of the average of total non-Omani salaries making up the difference between target and actual Omanization rates, though they are rarely enforced if the company is making good faith efforts to recruit Omanis. In addition, harsh penalties are applicable for transferring employment visa sponsorship from one individual to another or working under tourist visa status.

In a 2011 International Labor Organization (ILO) survey, 66 percent of survey respondents felt that current labor legislation is a constraint on enterprise growth. Only 13 percent of respondents believed that the local workforce has the necessary skills demanded by business, while only 9 per cent believed that Oman's tertiary and vocational education system generally meets the needs of the business community.

Oman is a member of the ILO. Oman has ratified four of the eight core ILO standards, including those on forced labor, abolition of forced labor, minimum working age, and the worst forms of child labor. Oman has not ratified conventions related to freedom of association or collective bargaining, or the conventions related to the elimination of discrimination with respect to employment and occupation.

Foreign-Trade Zones/Free Ports

The government has established free-trade zones to complement its port development projects investing heavily in the Duqm, Salalah, and Sohar Free Zones. These areas include strategically located ports and are well connected with modern infrastructure. An incentive package for investors includes a tax holidays, duty-free treatment of all imports and exports, and tax-free repatriation of profits. Additional benefits include streamlined business registration, processing of labor and immigration permits, and lower Omanization requirements.

Foreign Direct Investment Statistics

Systematic information on foreign direct investment is limited. According to PAIPED, FDI reached US $16bn at the end of 2011, and inflows were approximately US $2 billion during the year, double the preceding year's volume. In 2010, the most recent year for which a breakdown is available, data shows that the UK was the top source of investment at 33 percent (US $5bn), with the U.S. second at 20 percent (US $2.3bn) and the UAE third with 15 percent (US $2bn).

As per Capital Market Authority statistics from December 2009, foreign participation, including that from GCC nationals, equaled 23 percent in terms of shares held in the Muscat Securities Market. Foreign capital constituted 24 percent of the shares held in finance, 21 percent in manufacturing, and 23 percent in insurance and services. FDI has jumped over the course of the decade, from only RO 929 million, or US $2.4 billion, in 2003.

The largest foreign investor is Royal Dutch Shell Oil, which holds 34 percent of Petroleum Development Oman, the state oil company, and 30 percent of Oman Liquid Natural Gas. Other companies, such as Occidental Petroleum, BP Amoco, Novus Petroleum, Hunt, British Gas, and Nimr, have also invested in Oman's petroleum and gas sectors. U.S. firms, including Dover (oil drilling rods), VFT Global (controlled environment agriculture), Gorman Rupp (water pumps) and FMC (wellhead equipment), have entered into joint ventures with Omani partners. Since 1999, Oman has witnessed increased foreign direct investment through the privatization process. Major foreign investors that have entered the Omani market recently include Suez-Tractabel (France), Alcan (Canada), LG (Korea), Veolia (France), SinoHydro (China), and National Power (UK).

According to the latest statistics available from the National Center for Statistics & Information, in 2010 manufacturing received the lion's share of FDI, at 30.7 percent, with oil and gas exploration a close second at 28.1 percent, and financial intermediation at 23.6 percent. Most American FDI has been directed at oil and gas exploration (90 percent), with about 7 percent invested in manufacturing.

Web Resources

Ministry of Commerce and Industry
http://www.MOCIoman.gov.om/

Public Authority for Investment Promotion and Export Development (PAIPED)
http://www.ociped.com/

Public Establishment for Industrial Estates
http://www.peie.om/

Oman Chamber of Commerce and Industry
http://www.omanchamber.com/

Muscat American Business Council
http://mabcoman.com/

In: Oman: Conditions, Issues and U.S. Relations   ISBN: 978-1-62948-086-2
Editor: Sebastian Haas   © 2013 Nova Science Publishers, Inc.

Chapter 5

OMAN COUNTRY PROFILE*

U.S. Department of State

GEOGRAPHY

Area: About 309,500 sq. km. (approximately the size of the State of New Mexico). It is bordered on the north by the United Arab Emirates (U.A.E.), on the northwest by Saudi Arabia, and on the southwest by the Republic of Yemen. The Omani coastline stretches 3,165 km.

Cities: *Capital*--Muscat. *Other cities*--Salalah, Nizwa, Sohar, Sur.

Terrain: Mountains, plains, and arid plateau.

Climate: Hot and humid along the coast; hot and dry in the interior; summer monsoon in the far south.

PEOPLE

Nationality: *Noun*--Oman. *Adjective*--Omani(s).

Population (2010 census): 2.69 million.

Annual population growth rate (2009 est.): 2.0%.

Ethnic groups: Arab, Baluchi, East African (Zanzibari), South Asian (Indian, Pakistani, Bangladeshi).

---

* This is an edited, reformatted and augmented version of U.S. Department of State publication, dated January 5, 2012.

Religions: Ibadhi; Sunni Muslim, Shia Muslim, Hindu, Christian.

Languages: Arabic (official), English, Baluchi, Urdu, Swahili, Hindi and Indian dialects.

Education: *Literacy*--approx. 81% (total population).

Health (2009 est.): *Infant mortality rate*--17 deaths/1,000 live births. *Life expectancy*--73.8 years.

Work force: 920,000 total; *Agriculture and fishing*--approx. 50%.

GOVERNMENT

Type: Monarchy.

Constitution: None. On November 6, 1996, the Sultan issued a royal decree promulgating the Basic Statute, which clarifies the royal succession, provides for a prime minister, bars ministers from holding interests in companies doing business with the government, establishes a bicameral parliament, and guarantees basic rights and responsibilities for Omani citizens.

Branches: *Executive*--Sultan. *Legislative*--bicameral Majlis Oman (appointed State Council and elected Consultative Council). *Judicial*--Civil courts are divided into four departments: criminal courts handle cases under the penal code; family courts oversee personal status issues using Oman's Personal Status Law, which is based on Shari'a (Islamic law); commercial courts adjudicate business and commercial matters; labor courts oversee labor and employment cases.

Political parties: None.

Suffrage: Universal adult.

Administrative subdivisions: *Eleven governorates*--Muscat, Dhofar, Musandam, Al-Buraimi, Al Batinah North, Al Batinah South, Al Dhahirah, Al Dakhliya, Al Shariqiya North, Al Shariqiya South, Al Wusta. There are 63 districts (wilayats).

ECONOMY

GDP (2011 est.): 6.2 billion Omani rial ($16 billion).

Per capita GDP (2010): $20,855 (including 815,000 resident expatriate workers)

Real GDP growth rate (2012 est.): 4.8%.

Natural resources: Oil, natural gas, copper, marble, limestone, gypsum, chromium.

Agriculture and fisheries: (1% of GDP in 2010). *Products*--dates, bananas, mangoes, alfalfa, other fruits and vegetables. *Fisheries*--kingfish, tuna, cobia, shrimp, lobster, abalone.

Industry: *Types*--crude petroleum (not including gas liquids) about 865,000 barrels per day; construction (5% of GDP in 2010), petroleum refinery, copper mines and smelter, cement and various light industries.

Trade (May 2011): *Oil and gas exports*--$12.6 billion (47% of GDP in 2010). *Major oil markets*--China (41%), Japan (14%), India (14%), Thailand (11%), Korea (6%), Taiwan (5%). *Non-oil exports*--$3.12 billion: live animals (6%), mineral products (28%), chemical products (23%), plastic and rubber products (13%), base metals (14%).

Major markets (non-oil)--U.A.E. (16%), China (12%), India (11%), Saudi Arabia (7%), Taiwan (6%). *Imports*--$9.6 billion: electrical machinery (21%), transportation equipment (26%), prepared foodstuffs (4%), mineral products (8%), chemical products (8%), base metals (11%). *Major suppliers*--U.A.E. (28%), Japan (12%), United States (6%), Saudi Arabia (6%), India (5%).

PEOPLE

About 55% of the population lives in Muscat and the Batinah coastal plain northwest of the capital; about 215,000 live in the Dhofar (southern) region, and about 30,000 live in the remote Musandam Peninsula on the Strait of Hormuz. Some 815,000 non-nationals live in Oman, most of whom are guest workers from South Asia, Egypt, Jordan, and the Philippines.

Since 1970, the government has given high priority to education in order to develop a domestic work force, which the government considers a vital factor in the country's economic and social progress. In 1986, Oman's first university, Sultan Qaboos University, opened. It has continued to expand, recently adding a law college, and remains the country's only major public university. In total, there are about 25 public post-secondary education institutions in Oman, including technical colleges, teacher training colleges, and health institutes.

There are three private universities and 20 private post-secondary education institutions in Oman, including a banking college, a fire and safety college, a dentistry college, and business and management colleges. Most of these public and private post-secondary education institutions offer 4-year degrees, while the remainder provide 2-year post-secondary diplomas. Since 1999, the government has embarked on reforms in higher education designed to meet the needs of a growing population. Approximately 40% of Omani high school graduates pursue some type of post-secondary education.

In July 2011 the Government of Oman announced 500 new scholarships annually for study in the United States, as part of an overall program of 1,500 scholarships for the year for Omani students going overseas. These scholarships are guaranteed for the length of undergraduate study, including up to a year and a half of intensive English language study prior to entering a degree program. The government also recently announced a new graduate scholarship program to award 1,000 scholarships over the following 5 years for study in the U.S., Canada, U.K., Australia, Germany, Japan, and Singapore.

HISTORY

Oman adopted Islam in the seventh century A.D., during the lifetime of the Prophet Muhammad. Ibadhism, a form of Islam distinct from Shiaism and the "Orthodox" schools of Sunnism, became the dominant religious sect in Oman by the eighth century A.D. Oman is the only country in the Islamic world with a majority Ibadhi population. Ibadhism is known for its "moderate conservatism." One distinguishing feature of Ibadhism is the choice of ruler by communal consensus and consent.

Contact with Europe was established in 1508, when the Portuguese conquered parts of Oman's coastal region. Portugal's influence predominated for more than a century. Fortifications built during the Portuguese occupation can still be seen at Muscat.

Except for a period when Persia conquered parts of Oman, Oman has been an independent nation. After the Portuguese were expelled in 1650 and while resisting Persian attempts to establish hegemony, the Sultan of Oman extended his conquests to Zanzibar, other parts of the eastern coast of Africa, and portions of the southern Arabian Peninsula. During this period, political leadership shifted from the Ibadhi imams, who were elected religious leaders, to hereditary sultans who established their capital in Muscat. The Muscat rulers established trading posts on the Persian coast and also exercised a measure of control over the Makran coast (now Pakistan). By the early 19th century, Oman was the most powerful state in Arabia and had a major presence on the East African coast.

Oman Country Profile 93

Oman was the object of Franco-British rivalry throughout the 18th century. During the 19th century, Oman and the United Kingdom concluded several treaties of friendship and commerce. In 1908, the British entered into an agreement of friendship. Their traditional association was confirmed in 1951 through a new treaty of friendship, commerce, and navigation by which the United Kingdom recognized the Sultanate of Oman as a fully independent state.

When Sultan Sa'id bin Sultan Al-Busaid died in 1856, his sons quarreled over his succession. As a result of this struggle, the Omani empire--through the mediation of the British Government under the "Canning Award"--was divided in 1861 into two separate principalities--Zanzibar, with its East African dependencies, and Muscat and Oman. Zanzibar paid an annual subsidy to Muscat and Oman until its independence in early 1964.

During the late 19th and early to mid-20th centuries, the sultan in Muscat faced a rebellion by members of the Ibadhi sect residing in the interior of Oman, centered around the town of Nizwa, who wanted to be ruled exclusively by their religious leader, the Imam of Oman. This conflict was resolved temporarily by the Treaty of Seeb in 1920, which granted the imam autonomous rule in the interior, while recognizing the sovereignty of the sultan elsewhere. Following the discovery of oil in the interior, the conflict flared up again in 1954, when the new imam led a sporadic 5-year rebellion against the sultan's efforts to extend government control into the interior. The insurgents were defeated in 1959 with British help. The sultan then terminated the Treaty of Seeb and eliminated the office of the imam. In the early 1960s, the imam, exiled to Saudi Arabia, obtained support from his hosts and other Arab governments, but this support ended in the 1980s.

In 1964, a separatist revolt began in Dhofar Province. Aided by communist and leftist governments such as the former South Yemen (People's Democratic Republic of Yemen), the rebels formed the Dhofar Liberation Front, which later merged with the Marxist-dominated Popular Front for the Liberation of Oman and the Arab Gulf (PFLOAG). The PFLOAG's declared intention was to overthrow all traditional Arab Gulf regimes. In mid-1974, PFLOAG shortened its name to the Popular Front for the Liberation of Oman (PFLO) and embarked on a political rather than a military approach to gain power in the other Gulf states, while continuing the guerrilla war in Dhofar.

With the help of British advisors, Sultan Qaboos bin Sa'id assumed power on July 23, 1970, in a palace coup directed against his father, Sa'id bin Taymur, who later died in exile in London. The new sultan was confronted with insurgency in a country plagued by endemic disease, illiteracy, and poverty. One of the new sultan's first measures was to abolish many of his father's harsh restrictions, which had caused thousands of Omanis to leave the country, and to offer amnesty to opponents of the previous regime, many of whom returned to Oman. He also established a modern government structure and launched a major development program to upgrade educational and health facilities, build a modern infrastructure, and develop the country's natural resources.

In an effort to end the Dhofar insurgency, Sultan Qaboos expanded and re-equipped the armed forces and granted amnesty to all surrendered rebels while vigorously prosecuting the war in Dhofar. He obtained direct military support from the U.K., Iran, and Jordan. By early 1975, the guerrillas were confined to a 50-square kilometer (20-sq. mi.) area near the Yemen border and shortly thereafter were defeated. As the war drew to a close, civil action programs were given priority throughout Dhofar and helped win the allegiance of the people. The PFLO threat diminished further with the establishment of diplomatic relations in October 1983 between South Yemen and Oman, and South Yemen subsequently lessened propaganda and subversive activities against Oman. In late 1987, Oman opened an embassy in Aden, South Yemen, and appointed its first resident ambassador to the country. The northern tip of Oman, called the Musandam Peninsula, is strategically located on the Strait of Hormuz, the entrance to the Gulf, 35 miles directly opposite Iran. Oman is concerned with regional stability and security, given tensions in the region, the proximity of Iran and Iraq, and the potential threat of political Islam. Oman maintained its diplomatic relations with Iraq throughout the 1990-91 Gulf war while supporting the UN allies by sending a contingent of troops to join coalition forces and by opening up to prepositioning of weapons and supplies. In addition, since 1980 Oman and the U.S. have been parties to a military cooperation agreement, which was revised and renewed in 2010. Oman also has long been an active participant in efforts to achieve Middle East peace.

Following the terrorist attacks on the United States in September 2001, the Omani Government at all levels pledged and provided impressive support to the U.S.-led coalition against terrorism. Oman is a signatory of most UN-sponsored anti-terrorism treaties.

GOVERNMENT AND POLITICAL CONDITIONS

Sultan Qaboos bin Sa'id rules with the aid of his ministers. His dynasty, the Al Sa'id, was founded about 250 years ago by Imam Ahmed bin Sa'id Al

Oman Country Profile

Bu Said. Sultan Qaboos is a direct descendant of the 19th-century ruler, Sa'id bin Sultan, who first opened relations with the United States in 1833. Since his accession in 1970, Sultan Qaboos has balanced tribal, regional, and ethnic interests in composing the national administration. The Council of Ministers, which functions as a cabinet, consists of 31 ministers (but only 29 ministries), all directly appointed by Qaboos. The Sultanate does not have political parties, and new powers that were granted to the bicameral representative bodies in 2011, which allow proposing and amending legislation, do not provide for a fully independent legislature.

In November 1991, Sultan Qaboos established the Majlis al-Shura (Consultative Council), which replaced the 10-year-old State Consultative Council, in an effort to systematize and broaden public participation in government. Representatives were chosen in the following manner: Local caucuses in each of the 59 districts sent forward the names of three nominees, whose credentials were reviewed by a cabinet committee. These names were then forwarded to the Sultan, who made the final selection. Since then, reforms have permitted Omanis to freely run for office in contested elections featuring universal adult suffrage.

The elected Consultative Council serves as a conduit of information between the people and the government ministries. The Oman Council, of which the Consultative Council comprises one half, can approve or suggest amendments to legislation, propose legislation, convoke service ministers, recommend policy, and conduct studies on public policy. It has no authority in the areas of foreign affairs, defense, security, and finance. In early 2003, Sultan Qaboos declared universal suffrage for the October 2003 Majlis al-Shura elections. Two women were elected to sit with 82 male colleagues in those elections, which were observed to be free and fair. Roughly 194,000 Omani men and women, or 74% of registered voters, participated in the elections. Elections were held again in 2007 and 2011.

The appointed Majlis al-Dawla (State Council) acts as the upper chamber in Oman's bicameral representative body. As of 2011, Sultan Qaboos had expanded the Majlis al-Dawla to 83 members from 53.

In November 1996, Sultan Qaboos presented his people with the "Basic Statute of the State," Oman's first written "constitution." It guarantees various rights within the framework of Shari'a and customary law. It partially resuscitated long dormant conflict-of-interest measures by banning cabinet ministers from being officers of public shareholding firms. Perhaps most importantly, the Basic Statute provides rules for the royal succession.

Oman's judicial system is based on Shari'a--the Quranic laws and the oral teachings of the Islamic Prophet Muhammad. Traditionally, family courts fell under the jurisdiction of the Ministry of Justice, Awqaf, and Islamic Affairs (since divided into the Ministry of Justice and the Ministry of Endowments and Religious Affairs).

Oman's first criminal code was not enacted until 1974.

In 1999, royal decrees placed the entire court system under the financial supervision of the Ministry of Justice, though the 1996 Basic Statute ensures the independence of the judiciary. Also, an independent Office of the Public Prosecutor (formerly a part of the Royal Oman Police) and a supreme court were created.

Regional court complexes were envisioned to house the various courts, including the courts of first instance for criminal cases and Shari'a cases (family law and inheritance).

The country is divided into 63 administrative districts (wilayats), presided over by appointed executives (walis) responsible for settling local disputes, collecting taxes, and maintaining peace. Most wilayats are small in area, but can vary considerably in population. The 63 wilayats are divided into 11 governorates. The governors are appointed directly by the Sultan and hold Minister of State or Under Secretary rank. Walis, however, are appointed by the Minister of Interior.

Although Oman enjoys a high degree of internal stability, regional tensions in the aftermath of the 1980-88 Iran-Iraq war, 1990-91 Persian Gulf war, and Operations Enduring Freedom and Iraqi Freedom continue to necessitate large defense expenditures.

In 2006, Oman spent roughly $3.84 billion for defense and national security--over 33% of its public expenditures. Oman maintains a small but professional and effective military, supplied mainly with British equipment in addition to items from the United States, France, and other countries. British officers, on loan or on contract to the Sultanate, help staff the armed forces, although a program of "Omanization" has steadily increased the proportion of Omani officers over the past several years.

After North and South Yemen merged in May 1990, Oman settled its border disputes with the new Republic of Yemen on October 1, 1992. The two neighbors have cooperative bilateral relations. Oman's borders with all neighbors are demarcated, including a 2002 demarcation of the Oman-U.A.E. border that was ratified in 2003.

Oman Country Profile

PRINCIPAL GOVERNMENT OFFICIALS

Sultan, Prime Minister, and Minister of Defense, Foreign Affairs, and Finance--Qaboos bin Sa'id Al Said
Minister of Royal Office Affairs--Khalid bin Hilal al-Busaidi
Deputy Prime Minister for Cabinet Affairs--Fahad bin Mahmud al-Said
Minister Responsible for Foreign Affairs--Yusuf bin Alawi bin Abdullah
Minister Responsible for Defense Affairs--Badr bin Saud bin Harib al-Busaidi
Inspector General of Police and Customs--Hassan bin Muhsin al Shuraiqi
Minister of Interior--Sayyid Hamoud bin Faisal al-Busaidi
Ambassador to the United States--Hunaina Sultan al-Mughairy
Permanent Representative to the UN--Lyutha Sultan al-Mughairy
Oman maintains an embassy in the United States at 2535 Belmont Rd. NW, Washington, DC 20008 (tel. 202-387-1980)

ECONOMY

When Oman declined as an entrepot for arms and slaves in the mid-19th century, much of its former prosperity was lost, and the economy turned almost exclusively to agriculture, camel and goat herding, fishing, and traditional handicrafts. Today, oil and gas fuel the economy, and revenues from petroleum products have enabled Oman's dramatic development over the past 40 years.

Oil was first discovered in the interior near Fahud in the western desert in 1964. Petroleum Development (Oman) Ltd. (PDO) began production in August 1967. The Omani Government owns 60% of PDO, and foreign interests own 40% (Royal Dutch Shell owns 34%; the remaining 6% is owned by Compagnie Francaise des Petroles [Total] and Partex). In 1976, Oman's oil production rose to 366,000 barrels per day (b/d) but declined gradually to about 285,000 b/d in late 1980 due to the depletion of recoverable reserves. From 1981 to 1986, Oman compensated for declining oil prices by increasing production levels to 600,000 b/d. With the collapse of oil prices in 1986, however, revenues dropped dramatically. Production was cut back temporarily in coordination with the Organization of Petroleum Exporting Countries (OPEC)--of which Oman is not a member--and production levels again reached 600,000 b/d by mid-1987, which helped increase revenues. By 2000, production had climbed to more than 900,000 b/d; however, it declined to

98 U.S. Department of State

roughly 750,000 b/d for 2006. Now at 865,000 b/d, Oman is on track to reach its goal of 1 million b/d through the use of innovative enhanced oil recovery techniques.

Natural gas reserves, which will increasingly provide the fuel for industrial projects in Sohar and power generation and desalination plants throughout the Sultanate, stand at 24 trillion cubic feet. A liquefied natural gas (LNG) processing plant located in Sur was opened in 2000, with production capacity of 6.6 million tons per year (tons/yr), as well as unsubstantial gas liquids, including condensates. The completion of the plant's expansion in December 2005 increased capacity to 10.3 million tons/yr.

Oman does not have the immense oil resources of some of its neighbors. Total proven reserves are about 4.8 billion barrels. Oman's complex geology makes exploration and production an expensive challenge. Recent improvements in technology, however, have enhanced recovery.

Agriculture and fishing are the traditional way of life in Oman. Dates, grown extensively in the Batinah coastal plain and the highlands, make up most of the country's agricultural exports. Coconut palms, wheat, and bananas also are grown, and cattle are raised in Dhofar. Other areas grow cereals and forage crops. Poultry production is steadily rising. Fish and shellfish exports totaled $104.7 million in 2006.

The government is undertaking many development projects to modernize the economy, improve the standard of living, and become a more active player in the global marketplace. Oman became a member of the World Trade Organization in October 2000, and continues to amend its financial and commercial practices to conform to international standards. The country signed a free trade agreement with the United States in January 2006, which entered into force in January 2009. Oman continues to pursue, through the Gulf Cooperation Council (GCC), free trade agreements with a number of other key trading partners, including the European Union and India.

Increases in agriculture and especially fish production are believed possible with the application of modern technology. The Muscat capital area has both an international airport at Seeb and a deepwater port at Port Sultan Qaboos. The large-scale modern container port and free zone at Salalah, capital of the Dhofar Governorate, continues to operate at near-capacity levels. The government in early 2004 approved a project worth over $250 million to add two berths and extend the breakwater at the port. Port expansion with a focus on tourist cruise ships is underway at Port Sultan Qaboos, and a large industrial and container port and free zone is in operation in Sohar. A national road network includes a $400 million highway linking the northern and southern regions. The government also recently expanded passenger and cargo capacity at its main international airports at Seeb (Muscat) and Salalah, and will construct new airports at Sohar, Ras al-Hadd, and Duqm, where a dry dock recently began operations and a modern city and free zone are planned. In an effort to diversify the economy, in the early 1980s, the government built a $200-million copper mining and refining plant at Sohar. Other large industrial projects underway or being considered include an 80,000 b/d oil refinery, a large petrochemical complex, fertilizer and methanol plants, an aluminum smelter, and two cement factories. Industrial zones at Rusayl, Sohar, and several other locations showcase the country's modest light industries. Marble, limestone, copper, and gypsum may prove commercially viable in the future.

The Omani Government embarked on its seventh 5-year plan in 2006. In its efforts to reduce its dependence on oil and expatriate labor, the government projects significant increases in spending on industrial and tourism-related projects to foster income diversification, job creation for Omanis in the private sector, and development of Oman's interior. Government programs offer soft loans and emphasize the building of new industrial estates in population centers outside the capital area. The government is giving greater emphasis to "Omanization" of the labor force, particularly in banking, hotels, and oil and gas operations benefiting from government subsidies. Currently, efforts are underway to liberalize investment opportunities in order to attract foreign capital, such as updating the foreign investment law. From 1996-2008, Oman's non-oil exports grew at a compound annual rate of more than 20%.

Some of the largest budgetary outlays are in the areas of health services and basic education. The number of schools, hospitals, and clinics has risen exponentially since the accession of Sultan Qaboos in 1970. After the Arab Spring protests in early 2011, the Government of Oman authorized a 1 billion Omani rial ($2.6 billion) increase in social spending--including stipends for military and civil service employees and scholarships--along with new mandates for the private sector such as an increase in the minimum wage and a push to boost hiring of Omani citizens.

U.S. firms face a small and highly competitive market dominated by trade with Japan and Britain and re-exports from the United Arab Emirates. The sale of U.S. products also is hampered by higher transportation costs and the lack of familiarity with Oman on the part of U.S. exporters. However, the traditional U.S. market in Oman, oil field supplies and services, should grow as the country's major oil producer continues a major expansion of fields and wells. Major new U.S. investments in oil production, industry, and tourism

100   U.S. Department of State

projects in 2005 totaled several billion dollars. Negotiations on the U.S.-Oman Free Trade Agreement (FTA) were successfully concluded in October 2005; the FTA was ratified by the U.S. Congress and signed by President George W. Bush in 2006. It entered into force on January 1, 2009, providing further impetus to bilateral trade and investment by offering advantages such as exemption from duties, national treatment, and 100% foreign ownership.

FOREIGN RELATIONS

When Sultan Qaboos assumed power in 1970, Oman had limited contacts with the outside world, including neighboring Arab states. Only two countries, the United Kingdom and India, maintained a diplomatic presence in the country. A special treaty relationship permitted the United Kingdom close involvement in Oman's civil and military affairs. Ties with the United Kingdom have remained very close under Sultan Qaboos. Bilateral ties with China have also increased considerably since 2007, as trade between the two nations has expanded rapidly.

Since 1970, Oman has pursued a moderate foreign policy and expanded its diplomatic relations dramatically. It supported the 1979 Camp David accords and was one of three Arab League states, along with Somalia and Sudan, which did not break relations with Egypt after the signing of the Egyptian-Israeli Peace Treaty in 1979. During the 1980-88 Iran-Iraq war, Oman maintained diplomatic relations with both sides while strongly backing UN Security Council resolutions calling for an end to the war. Oman has developed close ties to its neighbors; it joined the six-member Gulf Cooperation Council when it was established in 1981.

During the Cold War period, Oman avoided relations with communist countries because of communist support for the insurgency in Dhofar. In recent years, Oman has undertaken diplomatic initiatives in the Central Asian republics, particularly in Kazakhstan, where it is involved in a joint oil pipeline project. In addition, Oman maintains relations with Iran, and the two countries regularly exchange delegations. Oman is an active member in international and regional organizations, notably the Arab League and the GCC.

Oman has traditionally supported Middle East peace initiatives, as it did those in 1983. In April 1994, Oman hosted the plenary meeting of the Water Working Group of the peace process, the first Gulf state to do so. From 1996-2000, Oman and Israel exchanged trade offices. Oman closed the Israeli Trade

Oman Country Profile 101

Office in October 2000 in the wake of public demonstrations against Israel at the start of the second intifada.

U.S.-Omani Relations

The United States has maintained relations with the Sultanate since the early years of American independence. A treaty of friendship and navigation, one of the first agreements of its kind with an Arab state, was concluded between the United States and Muscat in 1833. This treaty was replaced by the Treaty of Amity, Economic Relations, and Consular Rights signed at Salalah on December 20, 1958.

A U.S. consulate was maintained in Muscat from 1880 until 1915. Thereafter, U.S. interests in Oman were handled by U.S. diplomats resident in other countries. In 1972, the U.S. ambassador in Kuwait was accredited also as the first U.S. ambassador to Oman, and the U.S. embassy, headed by a resident charge d'affaires, was opened. The first resident U.S. ambassador took up his post in July 1974. The Sultanate of Oman opened its embassy in Washington, DC, in 1973.

U.S.-Omani relations were deepened in 1980 by the conclusion of two important agreements. One provided access to Omani military facilities by U.S. forces under agreed-upon conditions. The other agreement established a Joint Commission for Economic and Technical Cooperation, located in Muscat, to provide U.S. economic assistance to Oman. The Joint Commission continued in existence until the mid-1990s. A Peace Corps program, which assisted Oman mainly in the fields of health and education, was initiated in 1973 and phased out in 1983. A team from the Federal Aviation Administration worked with Oman's Civil Aviation Department on a reimbursable basis but was phased out in 1992.

In March 2005, the U.S. and Oman launched negotiations on a free trade agreement that were successfully concluded in October 2005. The FTA was signed on January 19, 2006, and entered into force on January 1, 2009.

In 1974 and April 1983, Sultan Qaboos made state visits to the United States. Vice President George H.W. Bush visited Oman in 1984 and 1986, and President Bill Clinton visited briefly in March 2000. Vice President Richard Cheney visited Oman in 2002, 2005, and 2006.

INDEX

A

abolition, 85
abuse, ix, 12, 30, 32, 46, 48, 50
academic performance, 78
access, 13, 14, 31, 32, 33, 35, 38, 42, 44, 46, 49, 50, 64, 70, 73, 78, 81, 101
accommodation, 83
activism, vii, 1, 9
Activists, 8
AD, 73
administrators, 39
advocacy, 50, 81
Afghanistan, 14, 22
Africa, 2, 64, 92
age, 6, 48, 53, 81, 85
agencies, viii, 9, 29, 45
agricultural exports, 98
agriculture, 52, 67, 73, 74, 86, 97, 98
AIDS, 51
Air Force, 13, 14, 15
airports, 64, 99
Al Qaeda, 19, 24
alfalfa, 91
Algeria, 80
ambassadors, 6, 12
anger, 9, 24
annual rate, 99
antidumping, 73
appointees, 6, 12

appointments, 8
aquaculture, 63, 67
Arab countries, 23
Arab world, 14
Arabian Peninsula, 19, 92
Arabian Sea, viii, 2
arbitration, 65, 70, 71, 72
armed forces, 51, 94, 96
armed groups, 25
arrest(s), 9, 32, 33, 53, 54, 67, 71
Asia, 26
assault, 46
assessment, 13
assets, 24, 77, 78
asylum, 25, 42
audit, 77, 78
authentication, 66
authority(s), viii, ix, 6, 20, 29, 30, 31, 32, 33, 35, 36, 37, 39, 40, 41, 42, 47, 50, 54, 68, 72, 80, 95
automobiles, 26
avoidance, 80
awareness, 78

B

Bahrain, 6, 14, 15, 23, 24, 25, 72
bail, 20, 32, 33, 34
balance sheet, 68
banking, 19, 70, 77, 91, 99

104   Index

bankruptcy, 67, 71
banks, 69, 70, 76
bargaining, 51
base, 4, 13, 14, 91
basic education, 99
basic services, 42
Belarus, 80
Belgium, 80
beneficiaries, 83
benefits, 9, 65, 72, 83, 85
bicameral Majlis Oman, viii, 29, 90
Bilateral, 80, 100
birth control, 46
births, 90
blame, 82
blogs, 38
board members, 76, 85
bonds, 77
bonuses, 82
border security, 33
borrowers, 77
breakdown, 86
bribes, 44
Britain, 9, 99
British military, viii, 2, 14, 15
budget surplus, 65
bureaucracy, 75
businesses, 53, 66, 73, 76, 77, 78
buyer, vii, 2

C

Cabinet, 5, 66, 97
Camp David, 100
candidates, viii, 6, 7, 8, 10, 29, 42, 43
capital expenditure, 75
capital gains, 67, 70, 72
capital goods, 73
carbon, 73
cattle, 98
caucuses, 95
cell phones, 11
censorship, 32, 36, 37, 39
Central Asia, 100
certificate, 68

challenges, 49
Chamber of Commerce, 66, 72, 76, 87
chat rooms, 39
chemical, 91
child abuse, 48
child labor, 53, 85
child pornography, 49
children, 4, 12, 36, 44, 46-50, 53, 59
China, 80, 86, 91, 100
Christianity, 61
Christians, 58
chromium, 91
CIA, 3
cities, vii, 1, 5, 20, 66, 89
citizens, viii, 2, 6, 10, 25, 26, 29, 36, 38, 42,
     43, 45, 46, 49, 53, 64, 68, 73, 83
citizenship, 24, 36, 47, 48
civil action, 94
civil service, 99
civil society, vii, 1, 10, 44
clarity, 81
clients, 19
climate, vii
closure, 38
Coast Guard, 33
coastal region, 92
coffee, 38
Cold War, 100
collective bargaining, 11, 51, 52, 81, 85
colleges, 91
commerce, 93
commercial, 14, 16, 19, 34, 64, 65, 68, 69,
     71, 73, 74, 75, 76, 77, 80, 90, 98
commercial bank, 19, 69, 76
commodity, 76
communist countries, 100
community(s), ix, 12, 22, 42, 43, 45, 49, 57,
     58, 62, 85
compensation, 35, 53, 54, 70, 83, 84
competition, 66
competitors, 74
complement, 85
compliance, 47, 54
compounds, 61
computer, 65

Index 105

conference, 23
confinement, 31
conflict, 25, 80, 93, 95
conflict of interest, 80
confrontation, 24
Congress, 15, 16, 27, 100
consciousness, 40
consensus, 20, 24, 92
consent, 92
conservation, 27
Constitution, 90
construction, 8, 14, 23, 52, 60, 69, 91
consumer goods, 64
consumer protection, 7
Container Security Initiative, 19
contraceptives, 46
controversial, 39
conversations, 27, 28
cooperation, 13, 21, 94
coordination, 20, 97
copper, 91, 99
Copyright, 75
corporate governance, 76
Corporate Social Responsibility, 78
corruption, 44, 79
cost, 16, 67, 73, 76
Council of Ministers, viii, 29, 43, 95
counsel, 35
counterterrorism, 17
countervailing duty (CVD), 73
country of origin, 54
covering, 40, 81
credentials, 95
crimes, 32, 33, 37, 38, 39
criminals, 34
criticism, viii, 2, 11, 36, 37, 39, 76
Croatia, 80
crude oil, viii, 2, 26
CT, 63
cultural norms, viii, 10, 29, 47
currency, 70, 80
curriculum, 50
customers, 26
cycles, 6, 12

D

damages, 35
danger, 40, 53
data collection, 17
deaths, 7, 8, 90
debt service, 70
decision-making process, 75
defamation, 36, 39
defendants, 32, 34, 35
deficiencies, 79
demonstrations, 7, 9, 30, 35, 37, 39, 78, 101
denial, 36
Department of Defense, 28
Department of Labor, 53
depreciation, 81
detainees, 32, 33, 35
detention, ix, 30, 31, 32, 33, 34, 38, 40
detergents, 74
devaluation, 81
development assistance, 27
dignity, 36
disability, 83
disappointment, vii, 1
disclosure, 44, 76, 80
discrimination, viii, ix, 10, 11, 12, 29, 45, 46, 47, 49, 50, 57, 58, 61, 85
diseases, 83
disposition, 75
distribution, 65
diversification, 99
domestic industry, 73
domestic issues, 42
domestic violence, ix, 12, 30, 46
dominance, 66
draft, viii, 6, 29, 67
duty-free treatment, 85

E

East Asia, 13
economic assistance, 101
economic development, 47
economic migrants, 42

economic performance, 7
economic power, 69
editors, 34
educated women, 47
education, 7, 12, 43, 47, 48, 49, 50, 65, 67, 73, 83, 91, 101
educational opportunities, 50
educational system, 64
Egypt, 23, 80, 91, 100
election, 5, 6, 8, 10, 11, 12
electricity, 66, 69
e-mail, 36
embassy, ix, 3, 13, 22, 25, 27, 57, 62, 94, 97, 101
emergency, 82
emigration, 41
employees, 45, 48, 51, 76, 79, 80, 83, 84, 99
employers, 11, 51, 52, 53, 81, 83
employment, 26, 36, 49, 50, 51, 53, 54, 64, 81, 82, 84, 85, 90
employment opportunities, 64
empowerment, vii, 1, 11
energy, 21, 26
enforcement, 19, 53, 67, 71
engineering, 65
environment, 64, 86
equality, 12
equipment, vii, 2, 13, 14, 15, 16, 17, 19, 26, 72, 74, 86, 91, 96
equity, 69
Eritrea, 42
ethnic Indians, 58
Europe, 92
European Union, 80, 98
evidence, 5, 7, 8, 35
exclusion, viii, 29
exercise, 21, 34
exile, 93
expenditures, 9, 96
expertise, 63, 71
exploitation, 49
export control, 19
exporters, 80, 99
exports, 26, 67, 77, 80, 85, 91, 98, 99

F

Facebook, 37
factories, 74, 99
faith, 58, 59, 85
families, 12, 76
family members, 33, 53
family planning, 46
FBI, 20
FDI, 86
fear, 22, 37
female genital mutilation, 46, 48
female prisoners, 31
fencing, 74
fertilizers, 26
FGM, 46, 48
films, 39
financial, 17, 19, 41, 44, 51, 65, 68, 70, 74, 76, 79, 80, 86, 96, 98
financial institutions, 70
financial records, 41
financial support, 74, 80
financial system, 19
fish, 98
fisheries, 27, 74, 91
fishing, 53, 73, 90, 97, 98
fixed rate, 80
FMC, 86
food, 52, 78
food production, 78
forage crops, 98
force, 10, 15, 47, 64, 90, 91, 98, 100, 101
foreign affairs, 37, 95
foreign aid, 24
foreign banks, 66
foreign companies, 71, 75
foreign direct investment, 86
foreign exchange, 73
foreign firms, 73
foreign investment, 63, 66, 70, 76, 99
foreign policy, viii, 2, 100
formation, 63
France, 80, 86, 96
fraud, 43
free trade, viii, 2, 98, 101

Index

freedom, vii, viii, ix, 10, 11, 29, 30, 34, 36, 39, 40, 41, 42, 57, 60, 85
friendship, 3, 20, 93, 101
fruits, 91
funding, 9, 14, 41
funds, 10, 15, 17-19, 25, 44, 70, 77, 78, 79

G

GDP, 3, 90, 91
GDP per capita, 3
gender gap, 47
gender identity, 50
geology, 98
Germany, 92
God, 59
google, 28
government procurement, 73
government revenues, 26
governments, 67, 93
grades, 60
grants, 17, 27, 51
growth, 85, 90
growth rate, 90
guidance, 46
guidelines, 81
Gulf war, 94

H

health, 40, 46, 49, 50, 54, 64, 65, 83, 91, 94, 99, 101
health care, 46, 49, 50, 64, 65
health services, 99
hearing loss, 55
hegemony, 92
height, 27
Hezbollah, 25
high school, 43, 92
higher education, 11, 12, 43, 63, 92
highlands, 98
hiring, 76, 81, 84, 99
history, 43
HIV, 46, 51

HIV/AIDS, 46, 51
homes, 36, 60, 61
horses, 9
host, 23, 78
hotel(s), 67, 99
housing, 47, 50, 65, 81, 83
human, vii, viii, 9, 10, 11, 17, 27, 29, 30, 31, 32, 35, 44, 45
human right(s), vii, viii, 9, 10, 11, 17, 27, 29, 30, 31, 32, 35, 44, 45
humanitarian organizations, 41
husband, 47
hydrocarbons, 27

I

identity, 60
illiteracy, 93
immigrants, 19, 31
immigration, 33, 85
imports, 26, 73, 74, 85
imprisonment, 49, 58, 67, 71
improvements, 69, 98
impulsive, 6
incarceration, 9
income, 67, 72, 99
independence, 7, 11, 34, 52, 93, 96, 101
India, 27, 69, 80, 91, 98, 100
individuals, viii, 29, 31, 32, 33, 34, 35, 36, 38, 39, 42, 45, 46, 66, 70
industry(s), 73, 74, 76, 91, 99
inflation, 67, 83
infrastructure, 64, 77, 85, 94
inheritance, 47, 67, 96
injury(s), 53, 73, 83
inspections, ix, 30, 54
inspectors, 54, 81
institutions, 5, 26, 47, 51, 91
insurgency, 93, 94, 100
integrity, 24
intellectual property, 70, 75
intelligence, 17, 19, 33
interest rates, 69
interference, 22, 43, 44, 60
international standards, 31, 70, 98

interoperability, 16
intervention, 46
intifada, 101
intimidation, 50
investment(s), vii, 3, 21, 63, 64, 66, 67, 70, 72, 74, 76, 86, 99, 100
investors, 63, 65, 66, 69, 71, 72-75, 84-86
Iran, viii, 2, 13, 14, 15, 20, 21, 22, 26, 28, 42, 80, 94, 96, 100
Iran Sanctions Act, 21
Iraq, 13, 14, 22, 28, 94, 96, 100
Iraq War, 13
Islam, ix, 11, 22, 57, 58, 59, 61, 92, 94
Islamic law, ix, 12, 34, 46, 57, 90
Islamic world, 92
isolation, 81
Israel, 23, 28, 100
Israeli leaders, viii, 2
issues, vii, viii, 2, 4, 6, 10, 14, 23, 51, 71, 77, 81, 90
Italy, 69, 80

J

Japan, 23, 91, 92, 99
Jews, 49
job creation, 99
joint ventures, 27, 86
Jordan, 22, 23, 40, 91, 94
journalists, 9, 37
judiciary, 34, 35, 96
jurisdiction, 71, 96
justification, 24, 25
juveniles, 53

K

Kazakhstan, 100
kinship, 79
Korea, 86, 91
Kuwait, 6, 15, 101

L

labor force, 84, 99
lack of confidence, 38
laws, viii, 9, 11, 12, 29, 35, 37, 39, 42, 43, 44, 51, 53, 54, 59, 67, 70, 71, 75, 76, 79, 85, 96
laws and regulations, 76
lawyers, 32, 35, 65
lead, 13, 39, 60
leadership, 10, 25, 40, 52
Lebanon, 61
legislation, viii, ix, 6, 9, 29, 50, 57, 58, 66, 85, 95
legislative authority, 43
leisure, 67
lending, 69, 70
letters of credit, 77
liberalization, vii, 1, 5, 6, 76
lifetime, 92
light, 91, 99
limestone, 91, 99
liquefied natural gas, 98
liquidity, 77
liquids, 91, 98
litigation, 72
loans, 27, 74, 77, 81
local community, 47
local government, 21

M

machinery, 26, 91
magazines, 37
Majlis al-Dawla, viii, 29
Majlis al-Shura, viii, 29, 52, 95
majority, 11, 34, 51, 54, 58, 64, 65, 75, 77, 78, 92
Malaysia, 80
man, 12, 23, 26, 40, 47, 64, 85, 96
management, 11, 27, 37, 63, 69, 79, 81, 91
manufacturing, 63, 67, 73, 77, 86
marches, 50
marketplace, 98

Index

marriage, 4, 36, 47, 48, 49
married couples, 46
materials, 19, 43, 60, 72
matter, 33, 40, 70, 82
Mauritius, 80
media, 8, 9, 11, 12, 34, 35, 37, 38, 39, 44, 47, 48
mediation, 52, 93
medical, 31, 32, 40, 48, 49, 53, 54, 66, 81
medical care, 48
membership, 6, 25, 60, 78, 80
mental illness, 43
messages, 36, 39
metals, 91
methanol, 99
Mexico, 89
Middle East, vii, viii, 1, 2, 10, 13, 19, 23, 27, 69, 94, 100
military, vii, 2, 6, 13, 14, 15, 17, 21, 22, 25, 26, 34, 42, 93, 94, 96, 99, 100, 101
military courts, 34
military exercises, 21
minimum wage(s), 7, 9, 53, 54, 64, 76, 83, 99
Ministry of Education, 50
Ministry of Endowment and Religious Affairs (MERA), ix, 57
mission(s), 14, 16, 22, 41, 52
misuse, 35, 44, 79
moderators, 39
modifications, 27
Moldova, 80
monetary union, 20
money laundering, 19
moratorium, 75
Morocco, 80
mortality, 90
mortality rate, 90
Muslims, 11, 19, 58, 59

N

narcotics, 16
national security, 33, 37, 96
nationality, 12, 41, 51

natural gas, 3, 21, 26, 91
natural resources, 94
negotiation, 51
Netherlands, 23, 80
NGOs, 41
noncitizens, 34, 47, 48, 53
non-citizens, 3
North Africa, 19, 69
nuclear program, viii, 2, 20
nudity, 39

O

Obama, vii, 2, 14
Obama Administration, vii, 2, 14
occupational health, 53
OECD, 67, 78
officials, ix, 4, 5, 6, 10, 11, 14, 22, 23, 25, 27, 28, 30, 39, 44, 57, 62, 78, 79
oil, 3, 9, 21, 26, 27, 30, 52, 65, 66, 77, 80, 83, 86, 91, 93, 97, 98, 99, 100
oil production, 97, 99
old age, 83
openness, 23
Operation Enduring Freedom, 14
Operation Iraqi Freedom, 14
operations, 14, 19, 22, 26, 72, 73, 78, 99
opportunities, 7, 9, 47, 50, 59, 65, 74, 99
Organization for Economic Cooperation and Development, 48
organize, 58
outreach, 23, 45
Overseas Private Investment Corporation, 80
oversight, 19
overtime, 53, 82
ownership, 11, 65, 66, 70, 82, 100

P

paints, 74
Pakistan, 19, 22, 80, 92
Palestinian Authority, 23
Palestinian uprising, 23

Index

parallel, 70
parents, 47, 48
patents, 75
peace, viii, 2, 23, 59, 94, 96, 100
peace process, 23, 100
penalties, 44, 45, 51, 53, 54, 81, 83, 85
percentile, 69
permission, 36, 74
permit, ix, 8, 11, 19, 30, 48, 60
Persian Gulf, vii, viii, 2, 13, 20, 21, 64, 96
persons with disabilities, 49, 50
petroleum, 3, 26, 52, 86, 91, 97
Philippines, 91
photographs, 38, 60
physical abuse, 55
pipeline, 100
piracy, 16
plants, 98, 99
pluralism, 61
police, 31, 33, 35-37, 39, 40, 44, 45, 46, 52
policy, vii, viii, 2, 6, 8, 20, 29, 47, 69, 95
political leaders, 92
political parties, 6, 43, 95
politics, 39
polyurethane, 74
Popular Front, 93
population, 2, 11, 22, 49, 58, 64, 89, 90, 91, 92, 96, 99
population growth, 89
Portugal, 92
poverty, 94
power generation, 98
precedent, 71
prejudice, 39, 59
preparation, 74
preparedness, 40
president, 3, 6, 7, 13, 20, 24, 35, 100, 101
President Clinton, 3
presumption of innocence, 34
prevention, 80
principles, 78
prisoners, 20, 31, 32, 33, 34, 35
prisons, ix, 30, 32
private enterprises, 50, 78
private investment, 66, 77

private schools, 60
private sector, 7, 26, 47, 53, 54, 63, 67, 69, 74, 76, 79, 81, 82, 83, 99
private sector employers, 47
privatization, 66, 76, 78, 86
producers, 73
professionals, 5
profit, 68, 82
profit margin, 82
project, 26, 72, 73, 82, 98, 100
proliferation, 17
propaganda, 94
propagation, 59
property rights, 64, 75
prosperity, 97
protection, 12, 42, 74, 75
provincial councils, 43
public employment, 65
public enterprises, 78
public expenditures, 96
public policy, 95
public sector, 7, 26, 64, 80, 81, 84
public-private partnerships, 66
publishing, 38
pumps, 86
purchasing power, 3
purchasing power parity, 3

Q

Qaboos, vii, viii, 1-7, 9, 10, 12, 13, 15, 16, 19, 20, 26, 29, 38, 58, 79, 82, 91, 93-95, 97, 98, 99, 100, 101
Qaboos bin Sa'id Al Said, vii, 1, 2
quality of life, 64
questioning, 39
quotas, 75, 76

R

race, 45
radio, 11, 37
Ramadan, 62, 82
rape, 45

Index

raw materials, 72, 73, 74
real estate, 77
recognition, vii, 1, 23, 61
recommendations, 9, 68, 80
reconciliation, 9
reconstruction, 22
recovery, 98
recurrence, 54
reelection, 20
reform(s), v, vii, 1, 4, 7, 8, 10, 40, 50, 69, 92, 95
refugee camps, 24
refugee status, 42
refugees, 24, 41, 42
Registry, 68, 75
regulations, 6, 47, 51, 53, 54, 59, 63, 75, 81
regulatory framework, 11
relatives, 48, 79
relief, 52, 80
religion, ix, 11, 45, 57, 58, 60, 61
religious groups, ix, 57, 58, 59, 60, 62
remittances, 70
renewable energy, 63
rent, 17
repression, vii, 1
reputation, 4
requirements, 51, 52, 54, 63, 65, 66, 67, 69, 73, 76, 80, 81, 85
reserves, viii, 2, 26, 97, 98
resettlement, 42
resistance, 83
resolution, 25, 36, 51, 59, 66, 71
resources, 3, 9, 77, 91, 98
response, vii, 1, 65
restrictions, ix, 11, 30, 38, 41, 46, 51, 52, 57, 60, 61, 69, 77, 94
restructuring, 67
retail, 81
revenue, 26
rights, 6, 10, 11, 17, 32, 35, 36, 41, 44, 45, 48, 49, 50, 59, 82, 90, 95
risk, 80
rods, 86
Royal Oman Police (ROP), ix, 30
rubber, 7, 91

rubber products, 91
rules, 59, 74, 76, 81, 94, 95
rural areas, 46, 48
Russia, 80

S

safe haven, 17
safety, 36, 53, 54, 55, 81, 91
sanctions, 20, 21, 44
Saudi Arabia, 15, 19, 22, 24, 25, 89, 91, 93
savings, 69
scholarship, 11, 92
school, 38, 45, 48, 50, 58, 60, 64, 67, 92, 99
schooling, 50
scope, 6
secondary education, 49, 91
secondary schools, 78
security(s), ix, 5, 7, 8, 10, 13, 17, 21, 24, 26, 30, 31, 32, 33, 34, 36, 38, 40, 42, 44, 51, 64, 76, 77, 83, 94, 95
security forces, ix, 7, 8, 17, 24, 30, 31, 32, 33, 40, 42
security services, 31, 38, 40
sensing, 14
sentencing, 19, 32
separatism, 24
September 11, 17
service provider, 38, 65
services, viii, 9, 15, 19, 29, 32, 46, 49, 65, 86, 99
sex, 49, 50
sexual abuse, 48, 52
sexual harassment, 46
sexual orientation, 50
sexually transmitted infections, 46
Seychelles, 80
shareholders, 76
Sharia, ix, 34, 57, 58
shellfish, 98
Shiite factions, 25
shrimp, 91
signs, 37
Singapore, 80, 92
skilled workers, 52
slaves, 97

Index

sleep deprivation, 31
small businesses, 53
small communities, 58
smoothing, 63
smuggling, 16, 21, 24
social class, 45
social events, 78
social network, 39
social order, 40
social responsibility, 78
social security, 9, 65
soft loan, 99
software, 75
solution, 36
Somalia, 42, 100
South Africa, 69, 80
South Asia, 58, 89, 91
South Korea, 23, 80
Southeast Asia, 52
sovereignty, 25, 93
specifications, 73
speculation, 75
speech, viii, 10, 11, 26, 29, 36, 38
spending, 8, 65, 99
Spring, 64, 99
Sri Lanka, 55
stability, 24, 94, 96
stabilization, 24
standard of living, 98
state(s), vii, ix, 2, 3, 6, 9, 11, 13, 14, 15, 19-28, 33, 35, 36, 38, 41, 49, 52, 53, 57, 58, 69, 86, 92, 93, 100, 101
statistics, 45, 46, 50, 86
steel, 73, 74
stigma, 48, 50
stock, 77, 80
Strait of Hormuz, 2, 21, 64, 91, 94
structure, 41, 94
subsidy, 93
succession, 4, 90, 93, 95
Sudan, 80, 100
Sultan of Oman, vii, 1, 92
supervision, 96
suppliers, 91
suppression, 40
Supreme Court, 9, 71

surplus, 65, 77
surveillance, 16
Swahili, 90
Switzerland, 20
Syria, 24, 25, 80

T

Taiwan, 91
tanks, 17
Tanzania, 80
target, 85
Task Force, 19
taxation, 67, 80
taxes, 21, 64, 67, 69, 80, 96
taxpayers, 67
teacher training, 91
techniques, 98
technology, 63, 70, 98
technology transfer, 70
telecommunications, 38, 66, 76, 78
telecommunications services, 38
telephone, 31
television stations, 11, 37
temporary protection, 42
tensions, 8, 94, 96
tenure, 12
territory, viii, 2, 21
terrorism, 16, 17, 19, 33, 94
terrorist attack, 19, 94
terrorist groups, 14
terrorists, viii, 2, 17, 19
Thailand, 80, 91
The Basic Law, ix, 57, 58
thinning, 24
threats, 52
time frame, 33, 42
Title V, 28
tourism, 49, 63, 67, 73, 99
trade, 11, 21, 23, 26, 27, 28, 51, 70, 72, 85, 98, 99, 100
trade agreement, 98
trade union, 11, 51
trademarks, 75
trading partners, 98

Index

113

traditions, 60
trafficking, 13, 19, 52
trafficking in persons, 13, 52
training, 14, 15, 16, 19, 49, 52, 63, 67, 73, 76, 85
training programs, 76
transactions, 19, 76, 80
transparency, 19, 64, 76, 80
transport, 17, 83
transportation, 64, 83, 91, 99
treaties, viii, 2, 80, 93, 94
treatment, 31, 32, 35, 46, 47, 54, 65, 67, 68, 73, 81, 100
trial, 31, 32, 34
Turkey, 69, 80
turnout, vii, 1, 6, 8, 37

U

U.S. assistance, 15
U.S. Department of Commerce, 67, 71, 73
U.S. military, vii, 2, 14
U.S. policy, 20, 23
UK, 86
UN, 41, 44, 45, 47, 71, 80, 94, 97, 100
unemployment rate, 46
UNHCR, 41
unions, 11, 40, 51, 52, 81
United, vii, viii, 1, 2, 3, 10-15, 20, 21, 22, 23, 25, 26, 27, 73, 80, 89, 91-101
United Kingdom, 80, 93, 100
United Nations, 12
United States, vii, viii, 1, 2, 3, 10-15, 20-23, 26, 27, 73, 80, 91, 92, 94-98, 101
universities, 91
updating, 67, 99
urban, 38, 58
urban areas, 38, 58
Uzbekistan, 80

V

vegetable oil, 74
vegetables, 91

Vice President, 101
victims, 45, 52
Vietnam, 80
violence, 24, 46, 50, 51, 78
violent behavior, 40
vision, 16
vocational education, 85
vote, 8, 12, 42
voters, 7, 8, 43, 95
voting, 6, 43, 50

W

wages, 51, 52, 54, 64, 72, 81, 83
war, 13, 93, 94, 96, 100
Washington, 3, 27, 97, 101
waste, 9, 78
waste management, 78
water, 23, 27, 31, 40, 78, 86
water resources, 27
wealth, 78
weapons, 15, 25, 40, 94
wear, 5, 60
welfare, 42, 65
wells, 99
West Bank, 23
Western countries, 81
withdrawal, 25
witnesses, 35
work ethic, 85
workers, 9, 11, 31, 33, 36, 37, 51, 52, 53, 54, 58, 66, 81, 82, 83, 85, 90, 91
workforce, 12, 64, 82, 84, 85
working conditions, 36, 52, 54
working hours, 52, 81
workplace, 47, 55, 82
World Bank, 67, 68, 69, 70, 71
World Health Organization, 44, 46, 49
World Trade Organization (WTO), 27, 66, 72, 74, 98

Y

Yemen, 19, 24, 42, 80, 89, 93, 94, 96